THE CALL TO DEEPER
INTERCESSION
The Process Of Going Deeper In Prayer

By
PROPHETESS CAROLYN H. WILLIS

Copyright © 2015 by Prophetess Carolyn H. Willis

The Call To Deeper Intercession

by Prophetess Carolyn H. Willis

Printed in the United States of America

ISBN 9781498423106

All rights reserved solely by the author. The author guarantees all contents are original and do not infringe upon the legal rights of any other person or work. No part of this book may be reproduced in any form without the permission of the author. The views expressed in this book are not necessarily those of the publisher.

Scripture quotations taken from the King James Version (KJV) – *public domain*

www.xulonpress.com

Lamentations 2:18-19 – "Their heart cried unto the Lord, O wall of the daughter of Zion, let tears run down like a river day and night; give thyself no rest; let not the apple of thine eye cease

Arise, cry out in the night: in the beginning of the watches pour out thine heart like water before the face of the Lord: lift up thy hands toward him for the life of thy young children, that faint for hunger in the top of every street."

TABLE OF CONTENTS

INTRODUCTION ix
CHAPTER I 13
    Growing Pains
CHAPTER II 23
    Intimacy With God
     Introduction
    Intimacy With God
    A Vessel of Brokenness
    Forgiveness
CHAPTER III 57
    The Art of Intercession
    The Birth of Intercession
    A Yielded Vessel of Intercession
    The Call to Intercede
    The Importance of Intercessory Prayer
CHAPTER IV 81
    God's Laborers of Love
CHAPTER V 84
    Identification and Agony
CHAPTER VI 91
    The Power of the Tongue
CHAPTER VII 95
    The Call

DEDICATION

I give the honor and glory to God for the knowledge, understanding, wisdom, and experiences I have had in intercession by the leading and guidance of the Holy Spirit. I dedicate this book to the Father, the Son, and the Holy Spirit. To the servants of God, the late Apostle Harry Das (who has gone to his original home in heaven) and Rev. Cora Das, whom God used as instruments in the early part of my life in the Lord to train and teach me about intercession. I give honor and glory to God for my family and friends that continually encouraged me to get the book released into the hands of the people of God. To my best girl friend, and co-laborer in the gospel, the late Joyce Reed, who has gone to her true home in glory. She allowed herself, unreservedly, to be an instrument used by the Holy Spirit, to pray me through some very rough times. There were numerous occasions when the enemy literally tried to kill me that my friend stood in the gap and interceded for me, and did warfare on my behalf. I thank God for her because the Lord gave her to me to be a true friend. To Lee Dickerson, whom the Lord gave to me as a big brother in-the-Lord, to speak faith to me when my faith was getting weak, and for transporting us (his sister Joyce Reed, and my sister Nebraska Herring (who is now Kelley)) to speaking engagements. To my big brother in-the-Lord and co-laborer in the gospel, Ronald Bailey, who encouraged me to press on and fulfill the destiny and purpose of God in my life. I could talk to him about things that I was going through in the gospel and he was there to listen and give counsel. I thank my friends Christopher and Doris Warwick for planting financial seeds in helping to get this book out. You were my ram in the bush that the Lord used to be a financial blessing to me to get this book out. I thank Doris for encouraging me to get the book out when my heart had grown weak. Without your constant encouragement, this book would have stayed on the shelf. I thank Apostle Betty Bigesby for being a true friend to strengthen me and pray for me and so many of the brethren of her church who showed the love of Christ in so many ways. I will always love them. They are a part of me forever. They are my extended family. I thank God for all of you, and many more who were there for me in other ways. May the Lord bless them tremendously, in every area of their lives, for they are true friends indeed.

INTRODUCTION

Just as there are different levels of growth in God, there are different levels of growth in intercession. A lot of saints who are intercessors do not understand a lot about what they are going through when they are in intercession. I pray that this book will give you insight as I share with you some of my intercessory prayer experiences in the Lord. The Holy Spirit is faithful to carry you through different levels in intercession as you yield yourself to him to guide you. The scriptures tells us in St. John 14: 26 "But the Comforter, which is the Holy Ghost, whom the Father will send in my name, he shall teach you all things, and bring all things to your remembrance, whatsoever I have said unto you." In Romans 8:26-27 states, "Likewise the Spirit also helpeth our infirmities: for we do not know what we should pray for as we ought, but the Spirit itself maketh intercession for us with groanings which cannot be uttered. And he that searcheth the hearts knoweth what the mind of the Spirit, because He maketh intercession for the saints according to the will of God." The Holy Spirit is our teacher (St. John 14:25). Let us allow him to teach us how to intercede. No one person knows everything that the Holy Spirit wants to teach us in prayer. We are all still growing and learning. I pray that you will allow the Holy

Spirit to renew your spirit man and allow the Holy Spirit to pour new wine within your spirit.

I have come to a place in my walk in the Lord, in which I had cried before the Lord and asked him to teach me all over again. I had learned so much about prayer and intercession, through other Christian materials, Christian teachers and preachers, that I knew there was something that was missing. I knew only the Holy Spirit could teach me. I came before my Father and asked that He teach me the way that was right, that was not tainted with impurities of man's intellect, and pride. My Father is so loving and caring, and He cares about us so much, that He did just as I had asked. It was as though I knew nothing. I was being taught for the first time in intercession. I pray that you will enjoy this book, but most of all, I pray it will ignite such a hunger within you to seek the Father's face with such a fervency, as never before.

The Bible states that the Holy Spirit will teach us in all things, I can truly say that the Holy Spirit is continually teaching me in intercessory prayer. I will only share with you what the Holy Spirit has taught me. Due to the vastness of readers and their degrees of growth in God, I will not share a lot of the deeper truths in intercession. For newborn readers, I do not want to lose any of you in reading this book. Therefore, I will speak as simply and plainly as I can. There is still a lot to learn in the area of intercession. I pray that what I have to share with you will help you. I pray that the Holy Spirit will unite your spirit to His Spirit and put such a hunger and thirst within you to come dine at the Master's table and drink of His cup. Open your spirit and allow God to illuminate your mind, soul, and spirit concerning His heartbeat.

I speak to those intercessors that have pulled back from their place of abiding in the Lord regarding intercession. Come back to your first love regarding intercession. The Lord has need of you. You who are

Introduction

more mature in the area of intercession, come back: for the Lord needs you to fall back in line with His Holy Spirit and began to teach and demonstrate, in the place of prayer and intercession, how and what the Lord is saying. The alarm has been sounded to alert the intercessors to begin to intercede again by the leading and guidance of the Holy Spirit. The Holy Spirit will strengthen you, as you put on your armor again and began to stand in the gap and intercede for the church, our nation and other countries. He needs you back on the frontline. You know who you are, and you know that you have been discouraged by the onslaught of the enemy and how the enemy has used our very own to try to destroy what the Lord was doing through us. The Lord is going to redress, redirect, instruct, and strengthen you. He has fresh new wine to pour into you for what is to come. Get back in line and heed the voice of the Lord.

I speak to the Bride of Christ all around. You have the intercessor living inside of you. That intercessor is the Holy Spirit. He will teach you how to lay yourself before the Lord, and allow the Holy Spirit to direct you as to what, how, and when to pray. The whole world is at odds. War is inevitable. War is happening all around. It is happening in the streets, in the homes, and on the jobs. The earth is rumbling because of the sins of the nations, the sins of the people. We are the army of the Lord. We are His hands and feet. The Holy Spirit is crying from within us, but are we sensitive to His cry? Are we sensitive enough to the pulling of the Holy Spirit within us to draw away and pray? You feel the groaning at times within you to pray, to weep, but sometimes you push it aside. We ignore the calling of the Holy Spirit telling us to pray. It is time for all of the children of the Lord to stop what we are doing, and go back into our prayer closet and learn the voice of the Holy Spirit. Ask the Lord to forgive you for ignoring His Holy Spirit and to begin to teach you all over again to pray as He wants you to pray. Lord help us, your people, your church, to be obedient to come aside when the nudging of the Holy Spirit is pulling on us to go pray.

May God's love and grace be with you, as you start out on the journey of intercessory prayer.

Prophetess Carolyn H. Willis

Chapter I
GROWING PAINS

I would like to share with you in this chapter about myself and how God would take a willing individual believer and turn their life into an intercessor for the world and not just an intercessor, but a prophetic intercessor.

One cold winter night in the south, as the sound of the cold wind pounded against the windows of the wood frame house that my family lived in, a beautiful little girl was born to Mary Elizabeth. As the mother looked upon the child and saw how wonderfully she was made, she did not know who this little one would grow up to be one day. The child they called Carolyn brought much joy to her as a baby, and much pain also as she grew older. That little one was me.

As I grew, I felt that no one loved me and with a constant feeling of rejection, I soon found myself developing the need to be and to feel loved. This made me a very rebellious child and I guess to get attention I ran away from home quite often. There was a void in my life and I didn't know how to fill it. Some people have a very strange way of showing and expressing their love for others, or maybe they are just afraid to show that tender, caring side of them. I believe my feelings were shared by other family members, but when feelings are suppressed for so long, after a while, you tend to just over look it.

In the warmth of a summer's day, I would walk by the river and see the waves dancing. There were many days I would walk alongside the river bank and talk to my heavenly Father. You see, even though there was rebelliousness in my heart, there was a longing to be closer to God, the Creator of all things, the Alpha and the Omega. Talking to the Lord gave so much peace inside, that nothing else seemed to matter. Many times, I would talk to God, pouring out my soul to Him. I would cry myself to sleep on the bank of the river.

My grandfather was a spirit filled Pentecostal pastor and my grandmother was a mother in the church. She was a praying woman but most of all she was prophetic. She knew things that were about to happen before they happened. It was my grandmother who taught me as a child about the Lord. I can remember the many things that my grandmother would tell me about the Lord and about life in general. Everyone looked up to her and many people came to seek Godly counsel from her. She had the most amazing wisdom, and that is what I admired about her the most. She knew how to get in touch with God. My grandfather, Jesse, would say to my grandmother at times, "Sarah, the Lord is going to use this child in a mighty way one day." At that time, I did not have complete understanding of what he was saying. As years passed, my grandfather became very ill and died. After his death, and as the years came and went, I found myself clinging to my grandmother for security and comfort. My mother could not spend as much time with us as she wanted to, because she had to work during the day and most of her evenings were occupied with the work on the farm.

My grandmother would take me with her everywhere she had to go. When Sunday morning came, I had the joy of going with her to church. As the years passed, my grandmother became ill and was confined to her bed for the rest of her time here on earth. Every Sunday morning she would lay in bed crying because she wanted to go to church, and it would break my heart every time to see her cry. Every Sunday morning my grandmother would make all of us sit down and watch Evangelists Oral Roberts and Rev. A. A. Allen with her on the television. As I watched how the Lord used these men to minister to the different needs of the people, I would cry and pray within myself, asking the Lord to heal my grandmother and raise her up from that bed. I prayed for God to use me the way he used those men because I did not want to see another person suffer the way that my grandmother was suffering. Every Friday evening, the church that my grandmother attended and was a member of, would come and hold services in our home. The house would be full of people, and my grandmother would lie in her bed and praise the Lord with everyone else. I was about ten years old when I decided to give my heart to the Lord. Needless to say, this pleased my grandmother very much. One Friday night, after praising and worshipping the Lord, my grandmother asked me to give a testimony as to what the Lord had been doing in my life. I remember hearing testimonies of the saints from grandmother's church, so I knew what testifying was, but that didn't stop the fear that seemed to rise up within me. After I had given my testimony, my grandmother laid there with tears in her eyes and said to me, "Ann don't every change, no matter what people may say or do to you, don't ever change." I didn't have the faintest idea what she was talking about. I know now that she was talking about my relationship with the Lord and staying real. No matter what lies that may be told on me to try to stop me and try to ruin my character and name, she was telling me to stay real with God and to be truthful with God.

I will never forget the autumn night in 1964 that my grandmother went home to be with the Lord. I believe in her heart, she knew that she was going home, because during that day, she would not eat a thing, and later on during the day before she drew her last breath, she asked the Lord to hold on just a little while. She lived long enough to say the entire 23rd Psalms and then said, "Now Lord, I'm ready." So my grandmother, my best friend, my beloved, Sarah Lee Herring, closed her beautiful eyes, and gave up the ghost. I thought that my whole world had collapsed around me. I was angry with God because he took my beloved away from me. I could feel that emptiness coming back that she had so beautifully filled with her love. The realization that I had no one to share my heart with and to protect me anymore, started to take root.

As the years passed, I grew colder towards the things of God. I was angry with God, and the world. At the age of 15, I started dating men twice my age and engaging in things that a normal 15 year old just didn't do. I became more rebellious and began hanging around the gangs and even dating the leader of one gang. During all those times, I knew that God's hand was on my life, for I could see how He had protected me from flying bullets and from not being raped. I could sense His hand drawing me back to Himself, but I wouldn't yield to Him. Instead, I kept running, thinking that if I gave in to him, He would take away the only things I felt I had left; my will and my freedom. I felt that He had already taken too much. Oh, how wrong I was to think that. I know now that all he wanted to do was to love me the way I had always wanted to be loved. I wanted some answers from God pertaining to my grandmother's death. I especially wanted to know why He didn't heal hear, since she did cry out to Him for healing. I just couldn't understand.

At the age of 18, two weeks after graduation from high school, I moved to Washington, D.C. to live. Not because I wanted to, but because I had no choice. My stepfather and I never got along. So right after graduation, he told me that one of us had to go and it wasn't him. My mother loved him and gave me money to come to Washington, D.C. At that point, I knew for sure what rejection was. I felt like an outcast from my own family. I felt for sure that she would tell him to leave. He was a mean, deceitful, and unfaithful husband to my mother.

In living in Washington, D.C., I had experienced a lot of things. Things that would make any other country girl move back home, but since I knew that I couldn't, I had to stick it out. There were good times and bad times, but through it all, I learned to grow up very fast in a fast city.

At the age of 21, I met and married a wonderful man, my knight-in-shining-armor. The man I thought would change my whole life. I thought that I could finally love someone and they would love me back, for who I was, and not for what I could do for them. I knew that deep down within me there was a woman who could be gentle, warm, and loving, but, who could also be very strong. I thought that my marriage was the answer to all my problems. I poured myself into my marriage, and literally worshiped my husband. Of course, as in any marriage, there was good and bad times. I remember the times when my husband and I would rush home from his parents because I wanted to watch Rev. Oral Roberts and Rev. Clen Dentin on television. Just sitting there and listening to them would make me cry. Every Sunday morning, I would watch the different evangelists on television, and seeing how the Lord would use them to lay hands on the sick to be healed, tears would begin to roll down my face. My face would be washed with tears, because of the longing deep within my heart to be used by God to pray for the sick as well. I would ask the Lord to use me also to minister healing to the sick and bring forth deliverance to his people.

On New Year Eve's evening of 1976, I had received a phone call from my husband telling me that he was not coming home because he was at a New Year Eve's party. I felt all alone; I mean really alone, depression had set in good. I cried and cried until my eyes begun to hurt. I talked to the Lord again and asked him to bring a change in my life, that I needed help. As I lay there in the bed, I had turned on the television and there was this program on called "The 700 Club." I saw them praying for different people on the television and the people were getting results. Then all of a sudden Rev. Pat Robertson said that there was a lady watching them on television who was under a heavy cloud of depression, that your marriage was not great, and most of all, I was left home alone this New Year Eve's evening. He said that God loves me and cares for me, and as a matter of fact, he has been watching over me and protecting me all these years. He had said a lot more, but then he said, "All of my answers are in Jesus, and would I give Jesus a try. Right then and there I lifted my hands up and repeated a prayer after him. For the first time I felt free, and all of a sudden I was in a bubble of bright light. I felt light as a feather, and I wept like a baby, telling the Lord how much I loved him and appreciated him. After that experience with the Lord, I still tried to do the things that my husband wanted me to do even though I felt a restraint from within me not to go to certain places or to do certain things. I had no church to go to, I tried visiting some churches but I knew that they just didn't have what I needed. You see, I did not want religion or a religious service. I wanted to be in the presence of God. I did not sense the presence of God in the church nor did I see the power of God in operation, so I stayed home. I went back to the night clubs with my husband and friends only for the Holy Spirit to draw me back in.

In April of 1976, I became very sick and had to be hospitalized. A week before I was to be released from the hospital, I was in great pain, and to relieve my pain I was given a pain medication that contained a drug in it that I was allergic to. Immediately, I had a reaction to the medication and had to be rushed into a nearby examining room on the floor. As I laid there on the table in pain, I could hear the doctor saying that they would have to do exploratory surgery." I could sense the darkness around me, and I knew that I wasn't going to make it. Everything around me seemed as if it was getting darker and darker and the presence of death was all around me. I didn't realize that the Lord had this under control. He had given me a bedside nurse who was not only a nurse, but a spirit filled Christian who interceded for me. When I had gained consciousness the next morning, I asked the nurse what the time was. Instead of a direct answer, she raised her hands and began praising the Lord, and giving God the glory. Confused by her reaction, I asked what had happened, and she stated that the doctor and nurses thought they had lost me for sure because my heart had stopped, and all of my vital signs were gone, but they did not give up. God sovereignly intervened again on my behalf. I thank the Lord for intercessors who will not hesitate to pray when they see a need.

I was released from the hospital at the end of that week and on 3 May 1976 I gave my heart to the Lord again. Oh, what a glorious day that was. My heavenly father loved me so much that he stuck by me through all that. In June of 1976, my husband told me that he wanted to leave. It was this that caused me to begin to seek God with all that was within me. I wanted my marriage to be saved as well as my soul, but I wanted my husband to come with me. We had always done things together as a team, and I wanted the two of us to come to the Lord together. The day came where I had to make a decision. It was hard, but I had no other chose but to let go and let God deal with him. I had no peace of mind, and I knew that the only answer to my problem was to yield to the Lord's dealing. My husband left me the second week of June. I was penniless, unemployed, and had no income. He paid my rent for a while, for which I am very grateful. My husband bent over and kissed me goodbye and left. All I could do then was to fall to my knees and began to pray for his soul, asking the Lord to give me a heart to forgive him and to love him as he loves him. Right then and there, I could feel the love of God engulfing me as a heat wave. It felt as though, God was literally pouring Himself into me and that a new heart was being placed where the old one was. I didn't hate my husband because I loved him so much, but this time it was a different kind of love. I prayed for his soul as if it was my own life at stake. At different times in prayer, God would give me a vision and I would literally see what my husband was doing. I would immediately begin to pray for his protection and ask God to spare his life. When he would come by to pick up his mail, I would tell him what the Lord had shown me in prayer, and it would startle him because he had to admit that it was true. The Holy Spirit had used me as an instrument in prayer to save his life from death many, many times because of the dangerous things he was involved in, and he himself will tell you that.

As a child growing up, I would have dreams about people, accidents, deaths, or whatever, and they would come to pass. Many times, God would give me dreams about people and things that were about to happen to them if they didn't take another route, and of course, the exact dreams that God would give me would come to pass immediately because they didn't believe in what I was saying. It had come to the point where I was told by many that if I had a dream about them to not let them know.

God had placed me in a church where I heard the word preached with the power and the anointing of the Holy Spirit. I saw the demonstration of the Word come to life, and God confirmed his Word with signs and wonders. The blind eyes were open, cancer disappearing, the deaf hearing, and the dumb talking. I saw people leaping from their stretchers dancing and running around the church giving the Lord glory. I saw God replace a metal plate in a knee with a knee bone right before my eyes, and I saw limbs grow. I knew then, that I was in the right place. What fascinated me the most is that they had prayer three times a day where the apostle of the church taught from the Word and shared the burden of the Lord. As he spoke from the Word of God, the burden of the Lord would come upon him and he would began to share the burden that was on his heart and in his spirit. He would have us to hear and catch the burden of the Lord. We would pray and literally prostrated ourselves on the floor or bowed our knees to the floor and prayed and travailed in prayer.

In 1977, my husband divorced me, and about two years later he remarried, and now he has a new family. I am still praying for him as the Lord places him on my heart, but I am also praying for his new family also. We parted in peace and as friends. I have found out through prayer that you do not have to separate as enemies. The world does that, but when you are changed by the power of God you can make the difference. I can truly say that if you want to be changed to be like Jesus, to have his character, and feel as he feels, it can happen, for that is His desire also, that we be like Him.

Through all of what I had experienced and what I had seen through the love of praying Christians, this caused such a desire within me to build a relationship with the Lord. A relationship built through the Word and in prayer. This was foremost in my life. As I drew closer to him in the Word, worship and prayer, he drew closer to me.

Chapter II

INTIMACY WITH GOD

INTRODUCTION

In Ezekiel 37 – The scripture states that "there were very many in the open valley; and, lo, they were very dry." These are souls that have died spiritually. Nothing seems to make them alive again. God asked Ezekiel, "Son of man, can these bones live?" And Ezekiel answered the Lord, "O Lord God, thou knowest." Again the Lord said to Ezekiel, "Prophesy upon these bones, and say to them, O ye dry bones, hear the Word of the Lord. Thus saith the Lord God unto these bones, Behold I will cause breath to enter into you, and ye shall live: And I will lay sinews upon you, and I will bring up flesh upon you, cover you with skin, and put breath in you; and you shall live; and you shall know that I am the Lord." So Ezekiel prophesied as he was commanded, and as he prophesied, there was a noise, and behold a shaking, and the bones came together, bone to his bone." Ezekiel looked and saw that muscle and flesh came upon the dry bones and that skin covered them all over but there was no life in them. The Lord told Ezekiel to prophesy to the wind and say to the wind, "Thus says the Lord God, come from the four winds, O breath, and breathe on these slain, that they may live." So Ezekiel prophesied as he was commanded, and breath came into them, and they lived, and stood upon their feet, an exceedingly great army.

Today, the Holy Spirit wants to breathe new life within you. He wants to pour new wine within you. Maybe there are some of you sitting reading this and you know that you are spiritually dry and spiritually dead. You don't have the vigor and strength, and joy that you once had in the Lord. Your soul has been crying out for a new fresh touch from God. I am here to tell you that God is here to meet you today. You must not hear or see with the carnal eyes and ears today, but hear what the Spirit of the Lord is saying to you. This day could be a day of new beginnings for you, if you allow the Holy Spirit to minister to you as He desires. Ezekiel 37:5 said, "I will cause breath to enter into you." The Hebrew meaning for Breath is Ruah which means wind or spirit. God is saying to you, today, that I am going to renew you with a new outpouring of my Spirit upon your life. "Old things have passed away, behold all things are become new (2 Cor. 5:17). The Holy Spirit will restore life into the deadness of your spirit. He will breathe life into the dead places of your life and cause you to become alive and anew in the Holy Spirit. He wants us as a people to know Him in the intimacy of His Holy Spirit. If you are reading this today and you are in that place, as those dry bones were, I am here to tell you that the Lord is going to breathe on your life by the winds of the Holy Spirit.

If you are thirsty today, I will say, "Come to the Living Waters. Do not waste your precious time digging wells that have no water in them" (Jer. 2:13; John 7:37). If you are hungry and you can't find anything to satisfy your hunger, then come. Come and be filled. If you are poor in spirit, I say to you, come. If you are afflicted and wounded, I say come.

If you are heavily burdened and the load is too heavy, I say come. You will be comforted and the burden lifted. Our Heavenly Father has his arms open wide to you. Throw yourself into his arms today. I speak to those who feel that you can't go any further because of the heavy trials that you are experiencing right now. The devil has tried to beat you into the ground and tell you that you can never be anyone special in the Kingdom of God. I speak to you to come. God wants you this day to experience Him in His presence and in His glory. In fact, the Lord has especially chosen you. You are the one most suited to know Him best. He loves you and cares so much for you, that you can't comprehend His depth of love for you. No matter where you are in Him today, come and dine at the Master's table and be fed by the Master's hand. He is standing there waiting for you. Just come into His presence and allow Him to love you as no one has ever loved you before. He is gentle, kind and full of mercy. Come now, says the Spirit of the Lord, and lose yourself in His bosom, that He may comfort you and share His heart with you. Come now, says the Spirit of the Lord and sit at the feet of Jesus. Allow the Holy Spirit to ease your mind and soothe your heart as you rest in His presence.

INTIMACY WITH GOD

Philippians 3:8-10
Psalm 42:1-2, 7; 63:1-2, 6-8; 143:6
Isaiah 26:9; Exodus 24:12-18; 33:9-11; 34:29-35

Psalm 42:1-2 – As the hart panteth after the water brooks, so panteth my soul after thee, O God. My soul thirsteth for God, for the living God: when shall I come and appear before God?

There is a special anointing that the Lord places on an individual who dares to stay holy before their Holy God. It only comes with a personal, deeply private encounter with the Holy Spirit. It continues and grows with a fellowship and communion that only you can establish through getting to know Him.

Give yourself to God so that He may do in your heart, what you have so long been a failure in trying to do. Acknowledge before Him His right to rule over you. As you come before the Lord, come with a pure heart of love. A love that is not seeking anything of itself, but only to give Him your total will. Only desire to please Him and to be a delight to Him so that you can be all His and void of self.

You know where I found the most joy? I mean unspeakable joy, peace, and strength. It is feasting at the feet of Jesus, just as Mary did when Jesus came to Lazarus' house. It is there that I found the love of a true friend. Every morning I would get up and say good morning to the Father, to Christ Jesus, to the Holy Spirit, and to my ministering angels. It is in this place of abiding that you build a relationship with the Holy Spirit. You see, I would talk to the Holy Spirit just as I would talk to you. He was faithful to share with me and show me many things. I have learned to depend upon Him, for my very life depends on His guidance and His friendship. My heart and my soul thirst after God. I long to see His power, and His glory as I have never seen before.

David said the same thing in Psalm 63:1-2 – "Oh God, thou art my God; early will I seek thee: my soul thirsteth for thee; my flesh longeth for thee in a dry and thirsty land, where no water is; to see thy power and thy glory, so as I have seen thee in the sanctuary." God wants you to know Him in His power and His glory. That is His heart's cry today. Oh to know Him, and to know the Holy Spirit. He wants to become your friend today. It is in this place of seeking and dying to self that we must come first, before the anointing. This is a place that you will not want to leave. This is the place of the Holy of Holies. This is a place where you say or do nothing. This is where you bask in His presence and receive from Him. This is a place where the "deep calls unto deep" (Ps. 42:7). This is intimacy with God and the Holy Spirit. This is where all you desire is to love Him, with all your being, and to know Him more intimately. I have been there so many, many times. That is why I can tell you that I am content in the state that I am in, in the Lord. I am content in the relationship and the intimacy that I have with my Lord, my friend and my love. This is a place where He can trust you with His anointing, with His secrets, and gems. Oh, brothers and sisters in

Christ, come and dine with Him. Come and love Him. He awaits your entrance. He has been waiting on some of you for some time now. Don't delay your coming. Come now, says the Spirit of the Lord.

Paul said in Phil. 3:8-10–"Yea doubtless, and I count all things but loss for the excellency of the knowledge of Christ Jesus my Lord: for whom I have suffered the loss of all things, and do count them but dung, that I may win Christ, and be found in him, not having my own righteousness, which is of the law, but that which is through the faith of Christ, the righteousness which is of God by faith: that I may know him, and the power of his resurrection, and the fellowship of his sufferings, being made conformable unto his death."

One definition of <u>know</u> is to be certain of; regard as true beyond doubt; to have a practical understanding of, or thorough experience with. The Hebrew definition of <u>know</u> is to possess knowledge; to know by experience; knowledge as a result of a prolonged practice; knowledge grounded in personal experience.

To know God is loving God more than anything or anyone. "Thou shalt love the Lord thy God with all thy heart, and with all thy soul, and with all thy strength, and with all thy mind...." (Luke 10:27).

Ask yourself these questions. Who am I in love with? Who means the most to me in my life? The proof of whether we love God will be demonstrated in our obedience to God's Word; and doing what He has told us to do.

When you love God with all your being, you will never have to worry about temptation. Why? Because the one that you are in love with, you will always put him first before yourself. In other words, you will not want or allow anything or anyone to separate or cause hurt to the one you love. You become very protective of the Lord's feelings. For when you have learned to love, you will not even desire to do those things that might offend the one you love. When you have learned to love Him, with all your mind, strength, and soul, you have then come to the real knowledge and understanding of what it means to be free in Him. This is the kind of love that Christ Jesus have with the Father. This is the kind of love that he portrayed about His Father while walking on the earth. Jesus was so one with the Father (St. John 10:30; 17:11, 22).

When you speak His name or hear His name, your very soul longs after Him. When you hear a sermon on the Holiness of God, your soul thirsts after Him. Just the very thought of Him causes your whole being to fall prostrate before Him and worship Him. Nothing else matters except to love your Father in the depths of your being, seeing Him as He really is, "Holy, Just, and True." This is what I will call "deep calleth unto deep." Once such love burns within your heart, you think of nothing else except how to please your beloved Lord.

In this place of abiding in His presence, you will learn to love God just because of who He is. Not because of what He has given you, nor because of His gifts, nor even for His precious presence. In this continual fellowship with the Lord, you will learn what it means to possess God. You are changed from glory to glory. As you possess him, you will inherit all his traits. This is godliness. The more you possess God, the more you are made like him (transformation). This is godliness that has grown from within you. If it is not from within, it is only a mask. The mere outward appearance of godliness is as changeable as a garment. But when godliness is produced in you from the life that is deep within you, then that godliness is real, lasting, and is the genuine essence of the Lord.

I Cor. 13:8 tell us that Charity never fails. Love cannot fail. Love will always strengthen you and give you the strength to push a little harder and to go a little further. In St. John 14:15, Jesus tells us—"If you love me, keep my commandments." Keep means to do. What the Lord is saying is this, if you love me, then you do what I ask you to do. In Phil 3:10 we see that Paul's heart desire was to know the Lord even more than he did. Paul's total dependence was on Christ. His primary aim was to know him. Paul had a glimpse of the glory of Heaven (2 Cor. 12:4). We need a glimpse of the glory of Heaven.

Saints, we really need a fresh touch from God. Those dead areas in our lives that was once full of the zeal and love of God need to be touched once again by the hand of God. That intimacy that we once shared with God needs to be rekindled. We must come back into the bed chambers of God Almighty. We must dine at his table. We must bask in his presence until we have experienced him as we have never before. Your very insides long for more of him. Your spirit touching his Spirit. His very thoughts becomes your thoughts. His heartbeat becomes your heartbeat. His eyes become now your eyes, and you no longer see through the eyes of the flesh. You now see through the eyes of the Spirit. His voice becomes your voice, and this is where true intercession comes forth, when you are in the Holy of Holies before the Lord.

Saints, do you know that there is a joy, unspeakable joy and peace that surpasses everything when you are wrapped up tight with the Lord. There is a satisfaction that comes from the relationship that you have with the Lord that you cannot get with a human being. Once this unspeakable joy and peace has been experienced, you can know the impossible in a special way. God desires my love and God desires your love. God wants you and I to really know him, as Jesus knows the Father, so should we know him.

There are those who are willing to pay the price that is involved in developing a personal relationship with the Father. You can be born again and do all the right things, such as working in the church, coming to all the services, paying your tithes, giving in offerings; and yet in doing all of that, you still do not know who He really is. God's ultimate goal and desire for all of us, is that we come to know him individually, and develop an intimate relationship with him. God wants his children to get to know him personally, so that we will take on his nature and character. It is this that brings manifestations of His glory.

God desires that his children know him to the extent that they are as comfortable in expressing their love to him as they are with their closest, most intimate friend here on earth. Only then will the children of God come to know the Father in the Holy Spirit.

In Matt. 7:22-23, it states, "Many will say to me in that day, Lord, Lord, have not we prophesied in thy name and in thy name have cast out devils, and in thy name done many wonderful works? And then will I profess unto them, I never knew you: depart from me, ye that work iniquity." Let us look at the words "I never knew you." This Greek word for "knew" is ginosko (ghinoceko) which means to "to know by experience or effort; knowledge as the result of prolonged practice; knowledge grounded in personal experience; to get to know." In essence, Jesus is saying, "I never got to know you, for you did not cultivate an intimate, loving, relationship with me." "You did not walk in total obedience to my Word. When the Holy Spirit began to pull on the reign of your heart to come and spend time with me, you ignored the tugging and did other things instead of coming away to be with me. I ask for quality time to be spent with me, so that we may fellowship with each other."

There is a place of deep anointing and deep intimacy in God that very few of us to get to know about. It is at this time that you are totally silent before the Lord, and all of a sudden you are caught up into glory.

Intimacy is only found in the Spirit—"God is a Spirit: and they that worship him must worship him in spirit and in truth" (St. John 4:24). This is a place we all have to come to, a place of intimacy that every part of our being is taken up into the presence of Almighty God. Our minds are in perfect harmony. Our bodies are in complete subjection, and our prayers are in the perfect will of God. And when you leave that place of sweet abiding to take care of your everyday responsibilities, you will not lose the presence of God.

Your knowledge of Him, your understanding of Him, your fellowship with Him reveals who He is; and you say, "I know Him better today than I did yesterday." I know more now than I did the day before how God is.

Paul is saying, I do not want to know about Him. Think of all the things we know about Him. But yet, do you know Him? Even if you could quote all the verses in the Bible and know every background history there was to know, yet that would not mean anything if I did not get to know the author of this Book personally and intimately.

Paul is saying, "all that I know, the knowledge that I have obtained through the reading of the Holy scriptures, the zeal that I had means nothing. All the human achievements that I had acquired means nothing; and the fame means nothing." He is saying, "I count all things loss for the excellence of the Knowledge of Christ Jesus." Paul's knowledge of Christ exceeds intellectual apprehension, but rather an experiential knowledge resulting from his personal communion with Christ. Paul wanted to know the Lord more deeply. He wanted a deeper inward relationship with Christ Jesus. It is only the turning over and yielding of your heart to the Lord. It is the expression of love within your heart for him. In Rev. 3:18—the Lord spoke and said, "I counsel thee to buy of me gold tried in the fire, that thou mayest be rich." This gold is much more easily obtained than you could ever imagine. It is available to you. How do I obtain it? You obtain it by building an intimate relationship with the one who gave his all so that you could have free access to Him (Jesus). It is when you allow the Lord to take you into the fiery furnace of trials, with the knowledge of who He is, and with a love so pure that you would easily yield to the dealings of the Holy Spirit in your life.

In your intimate time of prayer with the Lord, you will hear utterances beyond the power of man's ability to put into words, which man is not permitted to utter (2 Cor. 12:4). In this intimacy at times, you will have a paradise experience. Paul made the statement in 2 Cor. 12:2-4 – "²I knew a man in Christ above fourteen years ago, (whether in the body, I cannot tell; or whether out of the body, I cannot tell: God knoweth); such an one caught up to the third heaven. ³And I knew such a man, (whether in the body, or out of the body, I cannot tell: God knoweth); ⁴How that he was caught up into paradise, and heard unspeakable words, which is not lawful for a man to utter." Many times as I lay before the Lord in pray, I have had similar experiences whereas my spirit was in heaven talking to the Lord, and at the time it was as though it happened in a twinkling of an eye. At a blink, I was there talking to the Lord. I do not remember how I got there, and at that moment, I did not think about it. All that was important at the moment was my fellowship with him, listening to what he had to say, and receiving his instructions for my life. When you are in the presence of the Lord, your conscience does not think about how you got there, you are just there, and your spirit is there before the Lord. I hope that you understand what I am talking about. It is not spooky, we have got to get away from being so demon conscience all the time. When you are in the presence of the Lord, there is nothing but peace, joy and fulfillment. All that you are going through seems unimportant. As a matter of fact, you do not think about it. All that matters is that you have a desire to give everything over to the Lord. You become so submissive to the will of the Lord. Your only response to him is "yes Lord."

In Exodus 24:12-18, God wanted to talk to Moses more privately. The Lord told Moses to come up to him on the mountain and he would instruct him and talk to him. Moses went up onto the mountain and the cloud covered the mountain. The Glory of the Lord rested on Mount Sinai, and the Cloud covered it for six days. On the seventh day, God called to Moses out of the midst of the Cloud. The Glory of the Lord rested on the top of the mountain, and was like a consuming fire in the eyes of the children of Israel. So Moses entered into the midst of the Cloud and went up the mountain, and Moses was on the mountain 40 days and nights.

God wants us to come up into "HIS Mountain", and enter into HIS Holy of Holies and fellowship with him. This is where nothing else matters but what is actually happening between you and God. This is where you are endued with the power and the anointing of God. This is where God dwells. The only ones that can enter into the Holy of Holies are those who have been washed by the blood of the Lamb. This is a place where only the high priest can go. This is a place where only the born again can enter in. Unless Christ applies His blood to your heart, you cannot attempt to enter in. Moses stayed in the presence of God for 40 days and nights. In Exodus 33:11, the Word of God states that Moses spoke to God face to face, as a man speaks to his friend. In the 34th Chapter it tells us in the 29th verse that when Moses came down from Mt. Sinai from basking in the Glory Cloud of God, that Moses did not know that the skin of his face shone while he talked with the Lord. Because the people of Israel saw that Moses skin shone, they were even afraid to come near him, so much so, that whenever Moses spoke to the children of Israel he had to cover his face. Saints of God, how can your character and countenance not change when you spend quality time with the Lover of your soul. Moses spent quality time with the Lord. Not just 15 minutes, but quality time. That is why the Glory of God not only shown on Moses, but the power was manifested. That intimacy with God grows day by day as you walk with him, talk with him, and dine in his presence. The body of Christ needs to come back to that place so that the world may know that we are of Christ.

In Matt. 17:1-2, we read how that Jesus was transfigured on the mountain before Peter, James, and John. The scripture tells us that Jesus' face shone as the sun, and that his clothes were white as the light. The scripture tells us that while Jesus was in that transfiguration, that Moses and Elijah were talking with him. And in the 5th verse, it tells us that a bright cloud overshadowed them; and a voice came out of the cloud, which said, this is my beloved Son, in whom I am well pleased; hear him. Are you a son of God? Then I invite you to come to the Mountain and spend time with your Lord.

Saints of God, I am talking about relationship, being in love with God, not just talking about what you heard someone else say or what you have read. I am talking about having that one on one relationship. Who are you in love with today? Do you try to find love in people and other things? Are you seeking for love in all the wrong places? We always want someone to accept us, or we expect someone else to fill the void, that emptiness, and loneliness that we feel inside. That place, that void, and that acceptance can only be filled by God himself. Or ask yourself, why do I continually have those up and down syndromes? One day I am up and the next day I am down. It is only because you have not yet come into the reality of really knowing Him and the power of his resurrection, and the fellowship of his sufferings. Now this resurrection is not the power which brought about his resurrection, but it is the power which his risen life gives to those that are in him, victory over the flesh and the assurance of immortality (Rom. 8:11), a quickening and stimulating of the whole moral spiritual being.

When you have that relationship with God, and you really know the Father, whereas he is your life, your very being, your very reason for living, your very heartbeat, and your heart longs for him, then you will count all things loss for the excellence of the knowledge of Christ Jesus our Lord. David said in Ps. 42:1-2, "As the hart panteth after the water brooks, so panteth my soul after thee, O God. " Pants mean an audible long from thirst, almost in agony from thirst. It is an audible sound, a literal gasp for breath due to the longing of thirst. God moves when you are thirsty. "He that hungers and thirst after righteousness shall be filled," the scripture tells us in Matt. 5:6. You must be hungry and thirsty first in order to be filled. I am not talking about being filled with natural food, but I am talking about being filled with manna from heaven. Have you ever been in the presence of the Lord in prayer, where you are actually in heaven and when you come out, you feel full and you have no desire to eat natural food because you feel full? Why is this? It is because as you are ministering to the Lord, and as you offer sweet aroma to him that he in return feeds you in the Spirit.

David, Moses, Elisha, Elijah and all the children of Israel had the greatest opportunity of knowing the Father. God wants us to know him in the beauty of his Holiness. **"THAT I MAY KNOW HIM (Phil. 3:10)."** He was a friend to Abraham. God wants us to know him as our true friend. God wants us to know him in his power and his glory. In the outer court, my mouth is talking to God, in the Holy Place (inner court), my soul is talking to God, but in the Holy of Holies, my spirit is talking to God. Hallelujah, Hallelujah. David wrote in Ps. 46:10 – "be still and know that I am God." All that you want to do is love him with all of your being. This is what St. Luke 10:27 means to "love the Lord with all your heart, soul, strength, and mind." It is actually losing yourself in the bosom of God, losing your own soulish identity and taking on the identity of Christ.

Jesus prayed to the Father (John 17:3-5) and said, "And this is life eternal, that they might know thee the only true God, and Jesus Christ, whom thou have sent." Set aside a time to be with the Lord, turn your heart to the presence of God. Press through the Outer Court, the Holy Place, and enter into the Holy of Holies. Allow your spirit to enter into His chamber. This is where he dwells.

Having an intimate relationship with the Lord and the Holy Spirit will bring about commitment, humility, a teachable spirit and transparency. When I say transparency, I am saying that you are being totally open to the Lord, hiding nothing, and refusing to defend yourself. Get to know the third person of the trinity – the Holy Spirit, as a friend. He is the one that was left here on the earth to assist us, and to lead us and to guide us, and dwell in us. Never grieve the Holy Spirit. He has feelings too, and he can be easily grieved. But if you do, please always ask the Holy Spirit to forgive you. Let us make knowing Christ our main goal in life. Always pray in an honest and sincere manner, setting aside time to fellowship with him.

"Come away my beloved, and dine with me," saith the Spirit of the Lord.

A VESSEL OF BROKENESS

Matt: 16:24-25
"Then Jesus said to His disciples. "If any man will come after me, let him deny himself, and take up his cross, and follow me."
"For whosoever will save his life shall lose it, and whosoever will lose his life for my sake shall find it."

John 12:24-26
"verily, verily, I say unto you, Except a corn of wheat fall into the ground and die, it abideth alone: but if it die, it bringeth forth much fruit.
"He that loveth his life shall lose it; and he that hateth his life in this world shall keep it unto life eternal."
"If any man serve me, let him follow me; and where I am, there shall also my servant be: if any man serve me, him will my Father honor."

The only way that we are transformed is that there is an unveiling of our faces. The only way that we can be transformed is that there is an abandonment of self. The only way that you and I can be transformed is to absolutely die (dying to self). God has to cleanse his Church. He is going to cleanse us of every skepticism until we believe Christ. Christ is the head of the body, the church (Col. 1:18). God is going to have a glorious Church without spot or wrinkle (Eph. 5:27). God is going to come back for a virgin Church. A Church that is pure; one that has not laid down with other gods nor put on their garments, but one that is holy, without spot or blemish. God wants a Bride that will walk in virgin purity.

The Church has been polluted by ungodly methods and by all sorts of manipulations. We have been caught up in a religious system that literally has robbed us from seeing the glory of Christ. We have been so caught up with entertaining, we have forgotten about ministry. We have been caught up with activities to keep the people interested instead of showing them how to stay in love with Christ. The church should be open to allow the people of God to come in and cry out to God, repenting of their idolatry, pride, and greed; prostrating themselves before the altar, allowing the Holy Spirit to break them and melt them in his presence. If we moved back to this, we would see God's glory manifested in our churches and in our lives. It will take us coming to the end of ourselves, getting tired of the syndrome of everyday activities, and beginning to really hunger and thirst after God to bring about a change in us. Oh my people, who did hinder you from following after God with all of your heart? Where did your faith go? Where did your hunger for the Lord go? Where is the genuineness and the sincerity we once had towards the things of God? If we will come out and be ye separate, saith the Lord, and once again fall in love with Christ, we will see the manifestation of Him in our midst. If we walk and talk like the sons of God, with our faith becoming one with Christ, we will see him once again in our everyday lives. We will see him moving on our behalf and talking to us the way that he use to. We must be pure in heart and broken before our Lord.

It is vital that we be broken by the Lord. It is not that the Lord cannot bless the Church, but that the Lord's life is so confined within us that there is no flowing of the Holy Spirit through us. If the outward man remains unbroken, we can never be a blessing to his body, and we cannot expect the word to be blessed by God to flow through us. For the glory to flow through us there must be a death, burial, and resurrection in our lives. There must be that dying to self (our soulish man).

Do you know of the experience of having yielded your will to the Father? Not some of self and some of me, but none of self and all of me." God doesn't ask for golden vessels or silver vessels, but he ask for yielded vessels. He will take the most ordinary person and give that person wisdom beyond the wisdom of man. What courage and power you will feel that you can stand alone against the forces of hell. You will stand there strengthen and feeling like a giant, not standing in your own strength because you are drawing on unseen resources. This walk is real. This dying to self is real. You are no longer moving in self, but you are moving in the spirit. Gal. 5:16-17 tells us to "walk in the Spirit, and you shall not fulfill the lust of the flesh. For the flesh lusteth against the Spirit, and the Spirit against the flesh: and these are contrary the one to the other." Gal. 5:26 tells us not to be desirous of vain glory, provoking one another, envying one another. What idol is in your life that you are holding on to that you find difficult to let go? Let go of pride, anger, malice, maliciousness. Let go of lying, deceit, manipulation and control. Do you feel that you have to be in control all of the time? Do you have to control the conversation or anything else so that you can be recognized? You know a lot of us have such an ugly stink of pride operating in our lives that we can't see ourselves. All of these things can be dealt with in prayer if we would allow this flesh of ours to die to its own will and yield to the will of the Father in prayer. If we allow the Holy Spirit to deal with us in prayer about these things, then God would not have to allow these things to be exposed openly. God wants us to be vessels filled with his glory. We all are suppose to have the strength and the glory of God operating in our lives. We are to be containers or obtainers of the glory and the presence of God. God is looking for carriers of His power and glory. We must give our all to the Lord. Maybe some of our hindrances are the things that we have to deal with every day. There are things that traps us and bind us that are keeping us from doing what we know we should be doing for the Lord but can't because of weights and sins holding on to us down. The Lord is asking us to give it up so that we can be free to do his will. We must give ourselves to the Lord totally, not half, but all.

We must see ourselves as instruments being prepared by God for his service. We must come to the place in God where we will pray, "Lord let me not go untouched, unbroken, and unprepared. I must allow you to work in me what I have never dreamed of, so that I may become a prepared vessel whom you can use." A person who is mastered by God will never be mastered by anyone or anything. When Jesus walked on the earth in human form, he was not moved by people or things. He wasn't pushed into giving answers quickly or moving the way that the Pharisees and Sadducees wanted him to, for he said, "My meat is to do the will of him that sent me, and to finish his work (John 4:34). He was totally controlled by the Father, for he said in St. John 12:49-50 – For I have not spoken of myself; but the Father which sent me, he gave me a commandment, what I should say, and what I should speak. And I know that his commandment is life everlasting: whatsoever I speak therefore, even as the Father said unto me, so I speak. Jesus was totally yielded to the Father, and that is what the Lord is asking of us. Jesus wants us to be completely yielded vessels, totally dependent upon the Holy Spirit, totally dependent on the power of God. Without the Holy Spirit, we have nothing to give. Absolutely Nothing.

From the beginning of time, God created man in his own image, and he breathe into man the breath of life, the breath of the Living God (Ruah) and man became a living soul (Gen. 2). At that moment, man was created with a will, a will to choose right from wrong. Man chose to have his own will and disobeyed the Lord, and from that time on, man has been doing his own thing. From the beginning of time, God wanted a human being that would love him and obey him; one that would desire to do the will of the Father. God wants to change us. He wants us to be yielded to his will. You see, there are two wills, the will of God and the will of Satan. In Isaiah 14:13-14 – "For thou hast said in thine heart, I will ascend into heaven; I will exalt my throne above the stars of God: I will sit also upon the mount of the congregation, in the sides of the north: I will ascend above the heights of the clouds; I will be like the Most High." Four times, Lucifer said I will, I will, I will, I will. Do you see what I am talking about? When God created Adam and Eve, he gave them a will, a soul, and a spirit living in a body. From eternity pass unto eternity present, man and woman have been saying "I will" not the Lord's will, but "I will." God does not want robots to worship and obey him, but he wants people to make a decision to freely worship and obey him. From eternity pass and eternity future, we have the authority of God, or the rebellion of Satan; the will of God or the will of Satan; the will of God or the will of self. To live in the will of self is to be independent of God. To be independent of God means not to be dependent on God. There is no permissive will of God. We either <u>obey</u> or <u>disobey</u> (obedience or disobedience), submitting to the authority of God or submitting to the rebellion of Satan. We must choose this day whom we will serve.

Our spirit is released according to the degree of our brokenness. The one who has accepted the most discipline is the one who can best serve. The more one is broken, the more sensitive he is to the Holy Spirit. The more loss one has suffered, the more he has to give (for your bowels are full of compassion and mercy). Wherever we desire to save ourselves, in that very thing we become spiritually useless. The more you are dealt with, the keener is your perception of man. The more you are disciplined by the Holy Spirit, the more readily your spirit can touch another.

Hebrews 4:15 states that Jesus was tempted in all points, like as we are, yet without sin. The only way Jesus could identify with us in our sin was when he took our sin upon himself on the cross. Jesus is our greatest example of one that is disciplined by the Holy Spirit. And because of it, he touched many lives, and their lives were changed.

The Greek word for Cross is *stauros* (stow-ros') which means exposure to death, self-denial. Let us read Luke 14:27-35 – Brokenness brings about love, joy, peace, longsuffering, kindness, goodness, faithfulness, gentleness, and self-control. These are the fruits of the spirit that God wants to work in us. They are only produced in us by the crosses that we bare and by allowing the Holy Spirit to change us. We must come to that place where we can say "Lord I am going to take up my cross and follow you." That means that we are willing to die to self so that God may be glorified in our mortal body. What we are saying is not my will but your will be done. God wants to break our outer man (flesh). God sometimes has to strike us with a heavy blow in order for us to prostrate ourselves before Him and say: "Lord I dare not think, I dare not ask, I dare not decide on my own. In everything that I do and say, I need you (Prov. 3:5-6). For I truly see that I am nothing without you and I can do nothing without you (John 15:5; 2 Cor. 3:5). All of my efforts, works, and talents are worthless unless you control all of them." We must learn that our will is not to act independently from God.

When Jesus Christ was at the garden of Gethsemane, he gave up his will. He did not want to go to the cross in his flesh. He knew that in order for him to reign with his Father and his work to be accomplished on earth, it had to be the way of the cross. He had to put his will aside, for he stated, "not my will, but thine, be done" (Luke 22:39-42; Mark 14:36).

When we are broken, the outward man (flesh or will) is brought under the control of the Holy Spirit. The Holy Spirit is dominant. God's hand is upon us to break us – not according to our will, our thoughts, or our decision, but according to His will because we are not our own, for we were bought with a price, the price of the cross. Jesus had to go the way of the cross on our behalf because He loved us so much. We tend to blame others and get attitudes, when really all God is trying to get us to see is his hand cutting and shaping us.

In Genesis 32:24-28 – we read about Jacob wrestling with a man (his wrestling involved agonizing prayer) (Hosea 12:4). After Jacob was broken by the Angel (an Angel of God) he walked with a limp from that day on. All the people knew that he had been broken or dealt with by God, then the blessing of the Lord came and he had power with God and with man. He was no longer known as Jacob, the supplanter, the trickster, but Israel (prince with God), for he was a changed man. The old Jacob had truly passed away, for he was a new creature in the sight of God with a new name and character. He was a man that had been dealt with by God. From that moment on, we have not read that Jacob was a supplanter, and a trickster any more or shall I say still walking in that way.

One example of brokenness is the oyster. Before the oyster can be of use to you, you will have to break open the shell before you can get to the oyster. The oyster is of no value to you as long as it stays in the shell, but when the shell is broken and the oyster is prepared for eating, it will give off a good aroma and will taste very good to you. In this case, we are just like the oyster. We can't give off the sweet smelling aromas until our outer shell has been broken and then be prepared for service. In some of our lives, the Lord is able to accomplish this work after a few years of dealing with us, but for some others, it may take up to 15 years and the work is still unfinished. This is very serious because God could do the work in a shorter time span, but because of our will and attitude, we hinder God and stunt our growth in Him. This is why so many babes in Christ outgrow so many Christians who have been saved 10 to 15 years. Their spirit is so sensitive to the dealings and convictions of God, that they would prostrate themselves before God and allow him to do the work. An older saint would sometimes use his intellect to rationalize the dealings of God or ignore them all together. This is not the case 99% of the time. Please don't get me wrong, but the sensitivity and the tenderness that the babe in Christ may have by staying in prayer, the older saint might not have because they may have become relaxed and stagnant through the years and slacked in their prayer life. No matter how old we are in God, we must keep an open spirit to the Lord so that we may learn and grow.

In Luke 9:23 it states, "………if any man will come after me, let him deny himself, and take up his cross daily, and follow me." What it is saying is that you must set aside your own interest and gain, cleaving steadfastly to the Lord, conforming totally to His will, in living and dying if need be. Being broken by God is a continuous process as we give ourselves to God. Paul said that he died daily (I Cor. 15:31). It is dying to self, denying yourself of all the things and/or people who are pulling you away from God, and are causing you not to have that close intimate, personal relationship with the Father. Whatever or whomever they are, be willing to be freed from them. These entanglements will destroy you and separate you from your God. Let go of these weights and sins so that you may live. Even in our trials, we must yield to God. The quicker we learn, the quicker we will come out of the trial, not taking the trial grudgingly, but openly welcoming it. We must say as Jesus said, "thy will be done." We must be willing to be broken by the dealings and the hand of God, so that the work can be accomplished and the path that is laid before us can be completed and lives will be changed as we reach out to touch them. Ask God to show you the area in your life that is keeping you from having this relationship with him. Ask him to search your heart (Ps. 51:10-11; 139:23-24).

In Romans 9:20-23 we read of the potter and the clay. The potter is shaping the clay into a beautiful vessel, and if the vessel is not to the potter's likening, he would break and twist, adding little amounts of water onto it to soften and reshape the clay until it is just right. He may do this over and over many times before it is right. This is just how the Lord will do us, because He is the potter and we are the clay. Why? So that He might make known the riches of His glory on the vessels of mercy, which He had prepared beforehand for glory.

God is preparing us for change. He is getting us ready. God is saying, "I do not want you to look at someone else. No, I am dealing with you. I want to make myself known to you." You may say, "I know you Lord," but God will say, do you really know me the way that My Son Jesus knows me? That is what I want from you. For you to know me as my son Jesus does. I have said that you are my children and you are, but I desire that you come into my presence and see me in my glory that I may reveal unto you who I really am. For I am holy, pure, and I am just. I am a consuming fire (Heb. 12:29). In my glory you will lose your identity as the world sees you and you will now take on my identity. In my Word, didn't I say to you to be holy for I am holy (I Pet. 1:16). The world will no longer see you, but they will see me in you, in all my beauty, in all my majesty, because you have taken on my identity. You now talk like I do, you now walk like I do, you now love like I do, you now speak with authority and confidence of knowing who you are and of whom you are. The world now sees you in the fullness of my glory.

You can't come into the presence of the Lord and not be changed. He touches you in areas that no one else can nor have the power to. He comes that you might have life and have it more abundantly. How? Through brokenness by the Holy Spirit.

Maybe you are saying to yourself, "this is not easy to do, to allow the Lord to really break me, mold me, and reshape me into his image." I can truly and honestly say that God's grace is sufficient to take you through his refinery. Jesus Christ was so much man that it was difficult at times to believe that he was God, and yet he was so much God, until it was hard to believe that he was really a man. But he was God in man, with man, and for man. He was totally Jesus, totally God, and totally man. He was all that he said he was. He was a totally broken and yielded vessel or else he would not have been able to give his life on the cross. Please let us not frustrate the grace of God. Let us not cause his dying to be in vain. Jesus died once and for all. He did his part, now we as believers must do our part. We are workers together with him (I Cor. 3:9, 2 Cor. 6:1). As we walk with Christ, let us also identify with him. Let us open ourselves up to the Holy Spirit to deal with us in the areas of our lives that are displeasing to the Lord. If you live after the flesh, you shall die: but if you, through the spirit, do mortify the deeds of the body, you shall live (Rom. 8:13). In order for God to take us into deeper realms of the spirit, we must be emptied of all self, and allow him to retrain us and teach us as though we never knew anything. God is looking for yielded vessels today. He wants someone who he can talk to, walk with and speak through to a hurting world and say what the master wants to say to them. He is looking for channels to flow through to show forth his glory upon the earth. He is looking for vessels that are totally broken by God so that the inward man can be totally released. We must allow our spirit to be released, and when this happens, you will see the power of God flowing through you as you have never seen before.

I pray that God will be glorified in our bodies and that his Word will become alive and real within us. I pray that our understanding will be broadened and enlightened to understand who He really is and who we really are in Him. I also pray that we be made perfect in Him, speaking the same things, believing the same, that the world may truly know and see the Christ in us. Change us into your image and character, dear Lord. I ask these things in your Son's name, Christ Jesus. Amen.

Scripture Reading:

St. John 12:23-26	Romans 6:6; 8:16-17, 36	I Cor. 9:24; 15:31
2 Cor. 4:7-18	Galatians 2:20-21	Hebrews 4:12-13

FORGIVENESS

Matt. 6:14-15: "For if ye forgive men their trespasses, your heavenly Father will also forgive you." "But if ye forgive not men their trespasses, neither will your Father forgive your trespasses."

Rev. 2:7: He that hath an ear, let him hear what the Spirit says to the churches.

As we look at the times and seasons of our day, we can see the coming of the Lord nearer than ever before. But what is the Lord saying to the Body of Christ? In Rev. 2:4-7 – He is telling the body of Christ to go back to their first love and to remember from where they had fallen. He tells the church to repent and do the first works. Rev. 2 tells us about the loveless church, the persecuted church, the compromising church, and the corrupt church. Today we can see the same things happening to the church of God today. We spend so much of our energy fighting against one another, hating our brethren, being dishonest to one another, when the word of God tells us to love one another, to keep the unity of the Spirit in the bond of peace (Eph. 4:2-3).

Paul said in Ephesians 4:1-2 "I therefore, the prisoner of the Lord, beseech you that ye walk worthy of the vocation wherewith ye are called, with all lowliness and meekness, with longsuffering, forbearing with one another in love." Jesus tells us in Matt. 6:14-15 – "For if ye forgive men their trespasses, your heavenly Father will also forgive you: but if ye forgive not men their trespasses, neither will your Father forgive your trespasses." God Almighty is speaking to us from his word to forgive, to put aside our differences and obey the word of God. In Matt. 18:21-35 – It is talking about the unforgiving servant. Peter is asking Jesus how many times should he forgive when his brother sin against him. Jesus replied that he was to forgive him 70x7, and then Jesus goes on to tell them a parable about the kingdom of heaven being like a certain king who wanted to settle accounts with his servants. One of the servants owed the king 10,000 talents and was not able to pay. The king ordered that the man, his wife, his children, and all that the man owned be sold and that payment be made. The servant fell down at his master's feet asking for mercy, and to give him time to pay the debt. The king was moved with compassion, released him, and forgave him the debt. But the servant went out and found one of his fellow servants who owed him 100 denarii (which is $16 in U.S. Currency) and he laid hands on him and took him by the throat, saying, "Pay me what you owe!" So the fellow fell down at the servant's feet and asked for mercy but the servant showed no mercy and had the man thrown into prison until the debt be paid. Now his fellow servant became very grieved at what they had seen, they told the king and the king was very angry at the news. He sent for the servant and told this servant that he had forgiven him all the debt that he owed him because he begged him. He told this servant that he should have had compassion on his fellow servant, just as he had pity on him?" The king was angry, and had this servant sent to the tormentors until he should pay all that was owed to the king." Now this is very serious stuff here that Jesus is telling the disciples. Jesus' reply to them is this (v. 35) – "So likewise shall my heavenly Father do also unto you, if ye from your hearts forgive not everyone his brother their trespasses."

The reason that we do not forgive as much as we do is because we do not love the Lord as we say we do and we don't believe what his Word says. "If anyone say, I love God, yet hateth his brother, he is a liar: for he that loveth not his brother whom he hath seen, how can he love God whom he hath not seen" (I John 4:20-21)? And this commandment have we from him, that he who loveth God love his brother also. Love and forgiveness go hand-in-hand. If I really love you, then I can forgive a lot more. Take the woman who anointed Jesus' feet (Luke 7:47). Jesus said that her sins, which are many, are forgiven for she loved much. But to whom little is forgiven, the same loves little. (The scripture tells us that she continually kissed Jesus' feet and she anointed his feet with fragrant oil that was very costly. It did not matter what the worth of the oil was, she showed much love towards Jesus by kissing his feet, and anointing his feet with oil).

We are known to hold grudges, to be revengeful when God says that revenge is his, he will repay (Rom. 12:19). Romans 12:17 says – "Recompense to no man evil for evil." Proverbs 24:17-18, 29 states it this way: "Rejoice not when thine enemy falleth, and let not thine heart be glad when he stumbleth: lest the Lord see it, and it displease him, and he turn away his wrath from him." Twenty-ninth verse – "Say not, I will do so to him as he hath done to me: I will render to the man according to his work." What about the people that use us and mistreat us and spread all kind of malicious lies about us? What are we to do? Let us look at what Jesus had to say about this. In Luke

6:27-28, 31 – "But I say to unto you which hear, Love your enemies, do good to them which hate you, bless them that curse you, and pray for them which despitefully use you." Verse 31 says, "And as you would that men should do to you, do ye also to them likewise." Proverbs 25:21-22 – states it this way, "If thine enemy be hungry, give him bread to eat, and if he be thirsty, give him water to drink: for thou shall heap coals of fire upon his head, and the Lord shall reward thee."

If you can remember what happened and the pain is gone, then you have forgiven that person, but if the pain appears every time you think about it or talk about it, then you have not forgiven that person. In other words, every time you think about it or talk about it, you become angry and upset all over again, then you have not forgiven that person. When there is total forgiveness, you can share the experience and there is total joy while you are sharing it, then you are totally healed of that thing, because you have totally forgiven that person.

One of our first pieces of equipment or armor that we are to have on is found in Eph. 6:14. It tells us to gird our waist with truth (honesty). We must be honest with ourselves and stop trying to lie about how we feel. Isaiah 11:5 says "Righteousness shall be the girdle of his loins, and faithfulness the girdle of his reins." It is talking about the character of Jesus Christ. We are the bride of Christ. We are to be without spot or wrinkle, without blemish. Do we dare frustrate the mercy and grace of God? Do we dare grieve the Holy Spirit? Jesus left us here on earth to be his examples of His glory, to show forth his praise, to exemplify what the kingdom of God is really like. Matt. 5:23-24 – tells us about having unforgiveness in our heart toward our brother and trying to come to God to offer up prayers to him with that in us. He tells us to go make reconciliation. Go and ask forgiveness and then come back and offer up prayers unto him. How can we get our prayers answered?

Check your heart condition. When you are walking in right standing in God, you have prayer power, you are able to walk into the throne room of God in prayer and talk to the Master. Do you not know that every time we give place to the enemy, we have weakened our position of authority over the enemy? Why don't we see the enemy fleeing before us when we pray? We can't get our prayers answered if we are devouring one another with our tongues, this little member of our body. How can we get our prayers answered if we are bitter towards one another? Heb. 12:14-15 states it this way, "Follow peace with all men, and holiness, without which no man shall see the Lord: looking diligently lest any man fail of the grace of God; lest any root of bitterness springing up trouble you, and thereby many be defiled." We can't get our prayers through if we lie, not even a little white lie. A lie is a lie, no matter what color it is or how you try to dress it up, it is still a lie. We make a joke about it and say that we were just kidding when we know exactly what we were doing, lying. Rev. 21:8 says that all liars shall have their part in the lake which burneth with fire and brimstone. Revelation 22:14-16 says "Blessed are they that do his commandments, that they may have right to the tree of life, and may enter in through the gates into the city. For without are dogs, and sorcerers, and whoremongers, and murderers, and idolaters, and whosoever loveth and maketh a lie. I Jesus have sent mine angel to testify unto you these things in the churches. I am the root and the offspring of David, and the bright and morning star." So Jesus is talking to the Bride of Christ. Church, let us get our houses in order. We must present our bodies a living sacrifice, holy and acceptable to God, which is our reasonable service (Rom. 12:1). We must love without dissimulation (hypocrisy), abhor that which is evil, cleave to that which is good (Rom. 12:9).

Colossian 3:12-13 tells us to put on bowels of mercies, kindness, humbleness of mind, meekness, longsuffering, forbearing one another, and forgiving one another, if any man have a quarrel against any: even as Christ forgave you, so also do ye.

Christ came into the world to save souls, and he will reckon severely with those who hinder the progress of others who are setting their faces heavenward (Matt. 18:6). God is waiting on the bride of Christ to mature and to come into its place. We are the hindrance. God wants to come back but we are the hold up. I am talking about maturity in Christ. Church, we are in a battle, we are in warfare, not a battling against each other, but we are in a war battling against the host of hell. We are fighting against principalities, against powers, against the rulers of the darkness of this world, against a spiritual wickedness in high places (Eph. 6:12). Let's get our eyes focused in the right direction. We must fight to win. Don't let the enemy deceive you any longer, know his tactics, know his devices, know your enemy. 2 Corinthians 2:11 says that we are not ignorant of his devices. Let us not yield ourselves to be used by the enemy, but let us put on the whole armor of God and be the victorious army of God; that triumphant army of God here on planet earth. Let us serve the devil and his messengers notice today that we are going forth in victory, in power, and in the glory of the Lord. Let us tell him, no more will we allow him to use us to fight against one another, to be deceitful to each other, and to lie to one another. We are part of the army of God, we have gotten our marching orders and we have put on the armor of God and we are going forth now to do battle, battling against the host of hell and all his evil deeds.

Do you know that unforgiveness will lead you into areas of sin? What other sins are involved in unforgiveness: bitterness, rebellion, retaliation, resentment, hatred, rage, guilt, violence, anger, paranoia, and frustration. It is not what you eat that causes a lot of your problems, but it is what is eating you on the inside. It is medically known that ulcers are caused by the above actions. Unforgiveness can cause so many problems in our body.

If we live in a heart attitude that we will to forgive, and make it a part of our daily lives, then it will be easier each time to forgive, to the point that your heart and mind will be transformed to be like the heart and mind of Christ.

When Jesus was nailed on the cross at Calvary, he looked up to heaven and said "Father, forgive them: for they know not what they do" (Luke 23:34). Every stripe that he bore, every pain that he felt, every tear that dropped, the shame that he felt, and every drop of blood that was shed, all was taken because of forgiveness. He could forgive those who mocked and scorned him because he had the love of the Father living inside of him. We also have the love of the Father living inside of us. All the hatred that was tossed at Jesus, he took it and forgave them. Oh, what love was shown to them and that same love is shown to us. One day we shall behold him face to face, in all of his glory, and we all shall be judged of the things that we do to each other here on the earth today. Galatians 5:7 says, "Ye did run well, who did hinder you that ye should not obey the truth?" We must not give place to the enemy anymore, we must not.

We can't grow if we do not unblock the streams so that the waters can flow out freely and allow others to drink from the fountains in our lives. Unclog the flow, let the rivers flow, others are thirsty, let them drink from your fountain, let them drink from the rivers of Life that God has deposited within you. If you do not unblock the waters, it will become stagnant and begin to smell. But, we do not want that, we want fresh water, fresh new waters to flow through us, so that others may drink and live. God gives us newness every day.

Oh, God, I pray that what you have said will dig deep down in our spirit and will cause those things, those secret things, and those little foxes in our lives to be uprooted today. Allow fresh waters to begin to flow through us. Let there be healing in us and wholeness, for Lord, you seek for a whole church. A sick church cannot go out and heal a sick world. The body must be whole. We put aside all of our differences, and we ask that you forgive us for holding any kind of bitterness or unforgiveness in our hearts toward anyone. Create in us a clean heart, O God, and renew a right spirit within us. Cast us not away from thy presence, and take not thy Holy Spirit from us (Ps. 51:10-11, I am paraphrasing it to include all of the body). Do your work in us Holy Spirit, let us not leave the altar of prayer the same way that we came. We want to be changed, transformed to be like Christ, in Christ Jesus' name we pray. Amen.

Chapter III

THE ART OF INTERCESSION

There is a realm in the spirit that God wants to take us. It is the deep calling unto the deep. It is a realm in the Spirit of God where you are no longer walking in the flesh, but you are now walking in the spirit (Gal. 5:16). This is where the supernatural power of God is manifested. This is where we see and hear our God speak and give the orders. This is where we hear in the spirit, and move in the spirit. This is where we have open visions of what is actually happening. You are actually seeing in the spirit. This is a place in God where you know that you know because God has taken you there. It is a place where you only speak what your heavenly Father speaks. You do not lean on your own understanding, but you lean totally on God's everlasting arms. It is a place where you stand not in your own wisdom, but you stand in the wisdom of the Holy Spirit and you speak the mind of Christ. When you speak, you speak for God because the Holy Spirit is telling you what to speak. Your spirit has become one with His spirit. You speak in the power of the Holy Spirit which will change lives in the demonstration of the spirit and power of God. In I Cor. 2:4-5, Paul said: "And my speech and my preaching was not with enticing words of man's wisdom, but in demonstration of the Spirit and of power: That your faith should not stand in the wisdom of men, but in the power of God." We must move into this realm, where when we intercede, we only speak what is the heartbeat of the Father. This is prophetic intercession. The devil's aim to the body of Christ is to attack and conquer. Our mandate from God is to attack and conquer. Attack the enemy and overcome the wiles of the enemy, to conquer and live victoriously. How can we attack if we can't see or hear? We must learn how to walk in the spirit, and we must be trained by the Holy Spirit to follow him. We must train our ears to hear only what the Lord wants us to hear. How do we do this? Through prayer and the word of God.

Intercession belongs to the Church. In Acts 12:5 it says "and when the church prayed." Intercession has to come back into the church very strongly. Intercession has not gone into the depths that God wants it to go.

One reason why there is so much moral decay in America right now is because the American Church has backed off from the realm of intercession. When the Church did this, it allowed the devil to manipulate, deceive, and control her, which caused the Church to lose the glory and power that God had given her. Look at the state of the Church today. The power that Jesus demonstrated on the earth is not in the Church today. Jesus said in St. John 14:12-14 that "he that believeth on me, the works that I do shall he do also; and greater works than these shall he do; because I go unto my Father. And whatsoever ye shall ask in my name, that will I do, that the Father may be glorified in the Son." The Church has grown weak in its faith in Christ. Why? The 12th verse says that anyone who has faith in Christ will be able to do what Jesus did. Is this not what the Word of God says? If you have an intimate fellowship with the Father and you know Him, not knowing about Him, but really knowing Him, then how can your faith not grow in what He says in His Word? Let us bring it down to reality. How can I know you and trust you if I do not spend quality time with you on a consistent basis? You may tell me that you love me, but I will not believe it if I have not spent quality time fellowshipping with you, crying with you, praying with you, laughing with you, and getting to know your likes and dislikes. There would be some doubt there. Okay, let us take another example. You may be a member of a local assembly, and you have been faithful serving in your church for the past 20 years as a choir member, an intercessor, minister, and teacher. One day you look back at all the things that you have done in your church and you realized that your pastors has never taken the time to really get to know you. You have invited them to come to your events and they did not come for whatever reason. You needed prayer because of a serious illness, and you called the church to let the pastors know that you were very sick and needed prayer and had asked that one of them would call you to pray for you. Time passed by, days passed by, you never got a call or a visit. You went back to the doctor and were told that you had to have emergency surgery. You called again and told the pastor's executive that you were going into the hospital to have emergency surgery and would need prayer and again you did not get a visit or a call. You began to wonder if your pastors really cared about you. Why? There was no fellowship or quality time spent with you to really get to know who you were. Jesus states it this way, "I am the good shepherd; and know my sheep, and am known of mine (John 10:14). The Word of God tells us also to know those who labor among us (I Thes. 5:12). How can I know you if I do not spend time with you to get to know you? Do you see what I am saying? The Father wants quality time with His Bride, so that we can know the very essence of His heart. The Church has pulled away from that. How many people really do come out for prayer? The local assembly should have the same attendance on prayer night as it does on Sunday morning if not more. If we say that we love Him, then we would spend quality time with Him.

And I speak prophetically to you right now, "if the American Church does not accept God's intercession with travail and groaning of the Spirit, it will not see the great outpouring of the Holy Spirit. We will hear about it and we may see it happening in little spots here and there, but we will not see it in its entirety where it is poured out on all flesh. We will hear about the great outpouring of His Spirit in this particular city, state, or country and yet not see it happening where we are. Will God allow distress and persecution to come to the Church (the part of the Bride of Christ that is in America) in order to get us to seek his face and cry out for repentance for the sins of the Church as well as for America? This is what happened in the early church in Acts 8:1-4. God will do what he needs to do to get us to the place where we should be in order to do what we should be doing. My spirit cries out for the outpouring of God's Spirit to be poured out in this land, but it will not happen unless we go forth to battle now, through intercession, travail, and groaning in the Spirit. The Holy Spirit is crying out for the sons of adoption to cry out for this land, and our people. God will judge us, and He will judge America, if we do not come out of our comfort zones and seek the heart of the Father, and cry out for mercy for ourselves and for America concerning the lawlessness and immoralities that are going on all around us and in the church. Saints of God, we are in the last days, and God will shorten the days so that His elect will not be deceived (Matt. 24:22). Matthew 7:21-22 states that not everyone that says Lord, Lord, will enter the Kingdom of heaven, but he that doeth the will of my Father which is in heaven. I believe that there will be a remnant of believers that are living holy unto the Lord, and being faithful to the call of the Lord that will enter in. Lord help us to see, and hear what the spirit of the Lord is saying to the Church today."

We must come to know the person and work of the indwelling Holy Spirit. He is the intercessor (Rom. 8:26-27). He is the one who helps us to pray. He prays through us according to the will of God. We must realize that this type of prayer is more than praying in tongues, for what is spoken may be in tongues or in English. There are tongues that come out of your spirit to bring edification, but there are other kinds of tongues that are on a higher spiritual plane that comes by the Holy Spirit's direction and initiation. He takes hold of us to work together with Him. As this happens, we become more sensitive and can discern when the Holy Spirit is taking charge and directing our prayer. As we cooperate with Him, we can be assured that the will of God is coming forth and will be established in the earth. Ephesians 6:17-18 – gives us a clear picture of the help of the Holy Spirit in prayer and also in Romans 8:26-27.

Ephesians 6:17-18 – "And take the helmet of salvation, and the sword of the Spirit, which is the word of God: Praying always with all prayer and supplication in the Spirit, and watching thereunto with all perseverance and supplication for all saints."

Romans 8:26-27 – "Likewise the Spirit also helpeth our infirmities: for we know not what we should pray for as we ought: but the Spirit itself maketh intercession for *us* with groanings which cannot be uttered. And he that searcheth the hearts knoweth what is the mind of the Spirit, because he maketh intercession for the saints according to the will of God."

This is the rhema word, the word that the Spirit speaks. We can't pick a verse out of our promise box and expect to see the devil defeated.

It is not the logos word of God that will cause the enemy to flee. The word that worked for you the last time, might not work for you for this situation. The sword of the Spirit is the word revealed and made alive to you by the Holy Spirit. It is an exact word. It is a word of power and authority, with divine life breathed into it by the Holy Spirit. When the word is spoken out of your mouth, it causes heaven and earth to agree with you and move by the spoken directive word of the Holy Spirit and it will pierce the demons' ears and cause confusion. This specific directive word given by inspiration and revelation by the Holy Spirit will be the word of the Lord for that situation. The word that the Holy Spirit speaks will agree in principle with the written word of God. It will always line up with the character and nature of God. This is why it is so important to know the word of God and have it written on our hearts. We must be able to judge and discern what the Holy Spirit is speaking. When the word comes to us, it is not our word, but it is His word. You are His voice in the earth, speaking forth the will of God, that His plans and purposes will be established (Is. 55:10-51, Matt. 6:10). The word comes forth from God's mouth. It returns to Him, and shall accomplish what He plans. The word is carried by the Holy Spirit to our hearts. As we speak it, it returns unto God and becomes answered prayer.

Are you ready to move into the anointing of God to pray the heartbeat of the Father?

A. The Birth of Intercession

When I came to the Lord, I experienced different things happening in my life. One thing was when I had asked the Lord to give me his love, he gave me his compassion for souls. In order for the Holy Spirit to birth you with the heart cry of the Father, you must love souls. You must love them enough to want to see them free, no matter what the circumstance may be. Whether it may be sickness, stress, confusion, financial difficulties, or hurt, you must love enough to want to see them free.

For the first three months of my salvation, I was attacked almost every night by the enemy. At times my bed would shake. There would be an imprint of someone else being in the bed with me or a cat crawling on the bed with his paws going through the covers touching my legs. It was going through experiences like this that made me cry out to God for help. I asked the Lord to show me how to have victory over the enemy and to speak with authority and power against the power of the enemy. The Lord was faithful, for he taught me who I was in Christ, the position that I held in Him, and how to conquer the enemy. The Holy Spirit took me in prayer, in my prayer language, and began to teach me how to speak with authority to the enemy. He taught me exactly what to say and how to speak to the enemy. There are three things you must know. First, you must have a love for souls. Second, you must hate the devil and all his evil deeds. You must hate him with a hate that passes all hate. You can't have compassion for satan, because if you do, he has you deceived and you are already defeated. He will only laugh at you. Third, you must hate sin. Before the Holy Spirit can birth in you intercession, he must deal with you about things that are dear to you, and things which you are holding onto. You must not hold on to anything or anyone to the degree that you can't give them up. Now as a new born Christian, it will depend upon how much you yield yourself to the Lord. It will not happen overnight, for the Lord will continue to deal with us about things in our lives as we grow into the knowledge of who He really is. Once God has touched areas in your life, that only He knows needs touching, then you are ready to be used in intercessory prayer. We must realize that we are bridge builders, bridging the gap, serving the Lord and serving each other through intercession.

Intercession begins first with God, then through the Holy Spirit to us. Intercession and prayer must be a lifestyle. It must be as much a part of you as sleeping and eating. It is daily communicating with the Father, walking with Him, listening to Him, dining with Him, and sharing with Him. Jesus did it with the Father and we also can have that same lifestyle, the same fellowship with the Father. It is an emptying of self and being filled with more of Him. Asking Him, Lord what is your agenda for me today? What are my assignments, and who is in need of prayer today? Who can I intercede for and do battle for today? It is allowing yourself to be totally His.

As you make yourself available to God to use you in intercession, He will take you step by step into the deeper things of intercession. When I first came to the Lord (I was four months old in the Lord at the time), God took me through the channel of seeing in the spirit realm for whom I was praying for at various times. Later on as I progressed in the Lord, He took me further in the area of intercession. One thing that I must express is that intercessory prayer is in the area of helps. You are actually helping the Holy Spirit by allowing yourself to be used as a vessel for Him to work through in prayer (Rom. 8:26-27). The Holy Spirit makes intercession for the saints through the will of God. Who does He use? He uses you and I as instruments through prayer, intercession, supplications in the Spirit (Eph. 6:18, I Tim. 2:1). We are all **commanded** to intercede. Whom are we commanded to pray for? For all men, kings, and for all that are in authority. Intercession is what we all are supposed to do because we have the intercessor living on the inside of us. We are to aid the body of Christ with prayer and intercession. Intercessory prayer is for the whole body and not just for a selected few. As you read throughout the old testament, you will see how the people came together and cried out to God when they were in great opposition, or when they knew there was sin in their midst. In the New Testament, we read how the 120 were in the upper room praying together and how the power of God was poured out in such a great measure (Acts 1:12-14; 2:1-4). We also read how the church came together and interceded for Peter's release from prison, and how the chains were broken off of Peter, how the angel of Lord came and lead Peter out of the prison doors (Acts 12:1-16). Praise the Lord! That same power that was demonstrated then is the same power that can be demonstrated today. As we intercede for the nations, countries, and for the world, chains are being broken and prison doors are being opened. I believe that as we come together, everywhere, all over the world, and began to praise and worship the Lord and then go into intercession as the Lord begins to reveal his heartbeat to us, we will begin to see the mighty hand of God move upon this earth. We must be willing to be channels of the Lord, to allow the Holy Spirit to use us in intercession. As we draw closer to Him, we will see Him as He is, in his glory, His Shekinah Glory.

B. A Yielded Vessel of Intercession

True intercession is taught by the Holy Spirit, not by man. Man can give you their understanding of what the Lord has shown and taught them. In other words, they can only instruct you. It will take you getting down on your knees and asking the Holy Spirit to give you the burden. Then it is up to you to birth the burden once the Holy Spirit has impregnated you in your spirit.

You must count on God's faithfulness to show you and give you the scripture to pray for whatever He brings to your spirit. You must be attentive to the Holy Spirit in order for him to speak to you, or else you will not hear his voice or recognize his nudging. You must have confidence in God, in his word, and in the Holy Spirit.

Every born again, spirit filled believer can intercede before the throne room of God on another's behalf. I Timothy 2:1 tells us this. It also states that we should pray for other men, especially those who are in authority. We should also seek the throne of God to ensure that we may live a quiet and peaceable life in all godliness and honesty. In doing this, we can be assured that we are praying according to His will. For He delights in this kind of praying, for it is pleasing and acceptable to Him.

I must truly say that it is a joy to dine with my Father. It is a delight to stand in the gap for another soul. It isn't too hard to intercede on another's behalf. All God is asking is that you make yourself available. God is looking for Christians who would stand in the gap and make up the hedge (Ezekiel 22:30).

Let me share with you some of the wonderful delights in standing in the gap for another or shall I say, allowing the Holy Spirit, through you, to pray the heartbeat of the Father. Your spirit joins with the Holy Spirit and you began to lift up the needs that the Holy Spirit is showing you. Sometimes people who are close to individuals do not know what their needs are, but the Holy Spirit does. Let me give you an illustration. At the time you are speaking to someone, or you are involved in some other problem or situation, the Holy Spirit may nudge you in your spirit or let you know that someone is in need of prayer. At that very moment, you must obey the call of the Lord and begin to pray. Now, some of you may say that this takes time, but I am here to say that all it takes is your obedience to go and pray.

When I first came to the Lord, the Holy Spirit would come upon me to intercede. I would just obey and pray. As I prayed in the spirit, the Holy Spirit would enlighten my understanding, of what I was praying about, or the Holy Spirit would take me into a vision and show me exactly what was going on. For example, one day while I was at home, I had this tugging in my spirit to get on my knees and pray. As I got on my knees to pray, I began to weep, with gushing tears flowing down my face. As I was interceding in the spirit, the Lord had given me a vision of my sister. My cousin owned a funeral home in my hometown, and in the vision I saw him and his assistant coming to my home. My cousin was carrying a chubby, pretty, baby girl that looked just like my sister when she was a baby. I asked him why were they here. My cousin replied that they were there to pick up a body. Immediately I came out of the vision and began to weep vehemently, asking God to have mercy, for I knew immediately what it all meant. I began to plead for my sister's life and began to rebuke death. After I had prayed through, or shall I say until I sensed the release, I went into the living room and told my sister what the Lord had shown me in prayer. My sister knew it was God because just the night before, she had met death angels sent by satan. She knew that she had to make a sure stand then. My sister gave her heart to the Lord, in an open confession, and she is still serving and loving the Lord today. Praise God, Hallelujah! God is good. He is looking for someone who will say "not my will but thy will be done" in my life here on the earth today. We must love the Lord enough to lay down our lives for our brethren, he did it for us. "Greater love hath no man than to lay down his life for his friends" (St. John 15:13). We are the household of faith. We are to bear one another's burdens (Gal. 6:1-2). I was just a babe in Christ. The Holy Spirit will teach you and guide you into all truth (St. John 14:26; I John 2:26). God is a faithful God.

One thing I must stress and that is this. Whenever a person is interceding and you do not understand why the person is crying and crying so hard, please for the love of God, "do not touch the person in any kind of way." If you do not understand, then go find a place and pray yourself. A person's life is at stake and you may be the person who may cause his or her death. I know that this may sound hard, but I am dead serious. It is a very serious matter. The person interceding is in battle, in warfare for a soul and it is serious business. Please do not interfere. Please do not quench or grieve the Holy Spirit. Romans 8:26 says that the Spirit itself maketh intercession for us with groanings which cannot be uttered. The Holy Spirit intercedes through us with unspeakable yearnings and groaning. Think it not strange because it is not strange, it is a familiar function of the Holy Spirit in prayer. This is travailing in prayer, and to the human ears, it doesn't sound pleasant, but to an intercessor, it sounds heavenly. Paul travailed in birth for the Galatians until Christ was formed in them. He labored in prayer with deep groaning (Gal. 4:19).

There are so many realms in intercession in the Holy Spirit, but you will never get to know them if you don't open yourselves to the Lord and give yourself totally to Him.

We know a lot about the natural side of things, but we know very little about the things of God in the realm of the Spirit. We should get to know the Holy Spirit. I think that the Holy Spirit is the most ignored person of the trinity. We talk to the Father and the Son, we apologize to them but we seldom have a conversation with the Holy Spirit and apologize to the Holy Spirit. We grieve Him so much and yet how many times do we ask the Holy Spirit to forgive us? The scripture states that the Holy Spirit will teach us in all things. How many of us can truly admit that we allow Him to teach us? We live in a very intellectual society where knowledge is stressed in other things rather than the knowledge of God. We should know the Holy Spirit just as we know each other, even greater. A lot of things that God would show you in prayer are awesome. If you were not confident in this area of prayer, it would literally frighten you to the point of never wanting to pray again, because of the awesomeness of God. God will take you into prayer, praying His heartbeat, and actually showing you exactly that for which you are praying. The Holy Spirit is searching the hearts of men and women all over the world for 1) those who will say yes to His request to pray, intercede, and supplicate before the Lord, and 2) who will yield themselves to God, so that He can take them into the deeper things of intercession.

C. **The Call to Intercede**

Isaiah 66:8 says "……. for as soon as Zion travailed, she brought forth her children." I have learned what I do know about intercessory prayer through desperation. Intercessory prayer and the word was all I had to hold on to. Intercessory prayer is the foundation of any ministry, especially for anyone operating in the five fold ministry.

First, you may ask, "what is an intercessor?" An intercessor is one with genuine concern for others, who stands in the gap between man and God, making request before God and resisting the devil on man's behalf (Ezekiel 22:30-31; 32:9-14; Ps. 106:23; James 4:7-8). As we come to God, we are requesting that his hands move on behalf of the person, nation, or circumstances of our prayers.

Intercession is different from ordinary praying. In I Tim. 2:1 it states, "I exhort therefore, that first of all, supplications, prayers, intercessions, and giving of thanks, be made for all men." Here the Lord mentioned to pray and to interceded, therefore, we know that they are different. Moses made intercession for Israel (Exodus 32:11-14) and the Lord repented of the evil (judgment) which he thought to do unto his people. In verses 31 through 35 of Exodus 32, Moses laid down his own life for the people of Israel in intercession, he stood in the gap for them. He stated to the Lord, "if thou wilt forgive their sin; and if not, blot me, I pray thee, out of thy book which thou hast written." Moses loved the people of Israel to the point of dying for them. Because he interceded on their behalf, God did not destroy the whole camp but only those that had sinned against Him. Other scriptures to read about Moses interceding on the people's behalf are Exodus 33:12-18; Numbers 11:11-15; 14:13-19.

Other Old Testament intercessors were Abraham, Joshua, and Elijah. Abraham interceded for the righteous that lived in Sodom and Gomorrah (Gen. 18:22-23). Joshua interceded for the people because of the defeat at Ai, and not only Joshua, but the elders of Israel also (Joshua 7:1-26), and God had exposed the sin that was in the camp. God is faithful to show us and answer us if we are walking with him and obeying him. In Chapter 8 of Joshua, God gave them victory. In I Kings 17:17-24, Elijah interceded for the widow woman's son who had died. Verses 20 and 22 states that he cried unto the Lord, "O Lord my God, hast thou also brought evil upon the widow with whom I sojourn, by slaying her son? And he stretched himself upon the child three times, and cried unto the Lord, and said, O Lord my God, I pray thee, let this child's soul come into him again and he revived." How wonderful to know that God has some Moses, Abrahams, Elijahs and

Joshuas today who will also lay down their lives in prayer for God's people, for the nation and the world. Yes, and they are his people, who will count the cost, to let their souls be anguished and allow tears to flow, who will allow their heart to be burdened by the Lord for souls who are lost, hurting, and confused: intercessors, who will cry out to God for help for a world that is headed for destruction. If we do not humble ourselves and pray, what will happen to America? Most of all, what will happen to the Church?

As an intercessor, you will enter into the sufferings and take the place of the one prayed for. For example: there was a three-day retreat here in the Montgomery County region which I had attended. As we were standing in the line to get lunch, there was a sister that I knew, who I will call Sister One, standing in line sharing about the Lord. While standing there listening to what was said, I had an unction in my spirit from the Holy Spirit to go and pray with her. Now I had not spoken to this sister at all about what she was going through, neither had I spoken to her for some time. Sister One, and another sister, which I will call Sister Two, and I entered into the room in which Sister One was lodging. Another sister entered in the room by the name of Sister Three to pray with us. As I shared with Sister One the things that the Lord had shown me, we began to pray with her. As we began praying in the spirit, the Holy Spirit gave each of us what to pray concerning Sister One in English, then we prayed in the spirit again. Suddenly, the Holy Spirit began to impregnate me in the spirit with the burdens of Sister One. As I began to weep intensely, the Holy Spirit took control. I had understanding of everything that was going on in my surroundings. It felt as though my whole body was vibrating from the intensified weeping. I had to birth Sister One through her burdens. As I was in the process of birthing, I could feel everything that the Holy Spirit was doing. I was in pain spiritually and physically. I felt as if I were being electrocuted. I cried so loud that some of the others came to see what was going on. I knew that they must have thought that I was being delivered from demons, but I was birthing all that my dear sister was carrying for so long a time and could not release. It was just too heavy for her to carry alone, so much that she couldn't seem to give it to the Lord. It was so heavy, and that is just how I felt also, heavy.

As I interceded on my dear sister's behalf, I could sense that the Holy Spirit was releasing my sister. I prayed through. Praise God. The birthing process was completed. My dear sister cried so much and for the first time was able to weep before the Lord and release all that heavy load that she was carrying around for so long. She received a word of encouragement from the Lord, and she rejoiced, leaped, and danced before the Lord. Everything that was done and said, she confirmed it. From that day on, my dear sister was free from that bondage and she went on with the Lord with a new and fresh anointing on her life. She had accepted the calling on her life to minister the Word of God and moved with the Lord, with his anointing, ministering to many and seeing that they were made whole. You see, someone else had to stand in the gap for my sister in the Lord because she was too weak and too drained physically, and spiritually to do it on her on. I could go on and on with many more wonderful examples, but I think that you got the picture.

There are so many things that the Holy Spirit wants to share with us and show us. There are so many realms in the spirit that the Holy Spirit wants to take us, and there are many things that the Lord will show you about prayer that you will not be allowed to share. Why do we draw back from the Holy Spirit? We get to one place in prayer and stop because of fear. Don't you know that the Holy Spirit is here to guide us into all truth, and he will show us things to come (John 16:13). As we come into new areas in the Lord, we will begin to understand the move of the Spirit even more. As we stay in the word and move in the Spirit in prayer, God will give us many beautiful experiences in Him. I am not saying that these experiences may be delightful or pleasing to the flesh, but when you go through these experiences, you will know that God is doing a great work within you and through you. There are no special gifts, talents, or abilities needed to be an effective intercessor. The Holy Spirit has the gifts, and the talents. He will do the praying through you. All he seeks is a vessel to pray through. Allow the Holy Spirit to clean out every unclean thing in you. Then you will have great prayer power. As the Holy Spirit shows you areas in your life that needs cleaning or straightening out, or once he places his finger on that thing, bow down and repent before the Almighty God and be cleansed from it. Don't be like the dog going back to eat his own vomit. I know that this may be very hard to digest, but this is a serious matter. Do not take this lightly.

We have power to tread upon all the powers of the enemy. God wants his people to stand and use their authority in the Spirit of God over the enemy. He wants us to learn to operate in the Spirit along with his Word. God has given us the authority. We must realize this and begin to move in the Spirit of the Lord. By prayer and intercession, we can pull down strongholds. Move in the power of God through intercession. Know who you are in Christ. Know your position in the Lord. Know that you are a part of the army of the Lord. We are all told to put on the whole armor of God (Ephesians 6:10-18) to do battle. In verse 18, we are all told to pray always with all prayer and supplication in the Spirit. The Holy Spirit is calling all of us to prayer and intercession. We can send the Word of God to someone to break the powers of darkness over their lives through intercession, speaking the Word of God under the unction of the Holy Spirit. God is not hindered by distance. God is calling his people to come back to prayer and intercession. He never told us to stop praying. Jesus told his disciples in Luke 18:1 that men ought always to pray, and not to faint (don't give up, don't lose heart). The Word tells us in I Thes. 5:17 to pray without ceasing. That means to never stop praying. God is looking for his people to take the authority he has given them and use it. We have to put our eyes upon Jesus and allow him to show us how to see through his eyes. We must take the Word and be obedient in order for God to use us. God is not looking for intellectuals or philosophers. He is looking for ordinary people who will not give their ears to gossip and slander, but who will give their ears to hear his voice. He didn't give us ears to be used as garbage disposals. He wants us to walk just as Jesus walked. When we walked as Jesus walked we can move mountains. Once we walk in the power and the authority of God we can deliver ourselves through the Word of God. When you feel the release, you will know that the prayer has been completed. As you stay in your prayer closet in intercession, you will begin to see God move in your home, and the lives of your loved ones. Things that seem impossible become possible through intercession. You will see things changed. No matter what the circumstances may look like, you must be determined that you will press your way through intercession until you get a breakthrough. God will call you at various times of the day to intercede for situations, so that strongholds will be broken in the lives of others. It is time to quit playing church. It is time to take our place in the body of Christ and begin to really mean business with God. Souls are waiting. Souls are dying. Nations are waiting to be birthed through travail for their deliverances. Cities, states, countries and nations are in confusion, devastating situations are happening all over the land, and God is waiting for his body to begin to do battle in the Spirit. He is waiting for us to fall in line with his orders. Enough of fighting against one another. Let us turn all of that anger in the opposite direction, where it belongs in the first place, at satan and his empire. We must declare war on satan and his kingdom. We must hate the devil and what he stands for enough to war against him. Before the next outpouring of the Holy Spirit comes there must be a preparation of prayer and intercession. We the body must prepare the way for His coming.

As you look around, you can see the tragedy and turmoil surrounding this land and this world. When I hear about a child being beaten to death, or sexually assaulted, I would ask the Lord, was there an intercessor on the job. When I hear about someone being murdered, or a tragic accident where people have died, I have to ask, was there an intercessor on the job. When I hear of Christians tearing each other down because of doctrinal differences, causing the body to be torn apart, to be spotted and wrinkled, Lord have mercy, I have to ask, are there any intercessors on the job.

God is raising an army of intercessors who will say, no matter what the cost, I will lay down my life for the brethren and for the lost souls of men and women. God is raising a mighty army, skilled in battling in the spirit, who are not afraid. It is an army in the realm of the spirit. We are speaking mysteries that only God understands (I Cor. 14:2). That is why the enemy fights the intercessors so much because we are tearing his kingdom down. We are wrapping his hands and feet in chains and he can't move. There is an anointing that comes upon you when you are interceding in the Spirit. It is like fire coming down from heaven. You have the boldness, strength, and power to do the job, and bring it to completeness through intercession.

As intercessors we must learn that God is training us to hear His voice with distinctiveness and clarity. We do not listen to the clamors around us, but we listen to the voice of God. We are being trained by the master of all masters to be skillful soldiers of war, not warriors of the flesh, but warriors of the Spirit, the Spirit of God. No man can touch what God is doing. God shows the intercessors, through intercession, things that others do not yet see. He shows them things in the present and future. He instructs them when and how to pray. It is the cry in the spirit realm, the deep calling unto the deep, a sound that is heard in the heavenlies. All heaven is attentive to the cry of the intercessors. Demons are shaking in their boots, when the intercessors gather together to war against the powers of darkness, for they know that they are powerless. All the host of heaven looks on as the intercessors battle in the Spirit against the powers of darkness. There comes Michael to assist. The hand of the Almighty God is pushing back the walls of hindrances, grief, sorrow, sickness, diseases poverty, lack, despair, hopelessness, fear, doubt, and least among all, death. Oh, I wish that the children of God could see the mighty battle that is going on in the heavenlies as the intercessors are at war. What victories are being won.

Every prayer prayed in the spirit is prayer in the will of God. This prayer will be answered. It has the authority of heaven behind it, and a host of the angelic armies to bring it to pass. Your intercessory, travailing prayer will start the armies of heaven's angels marching. God is calling for people to yield themselves to become his prayer vessels, his channels to pray through.

Joel 1:13 – "Howl ye ministers of the altar." Howl comes from the Hebrew word Yalal (Yaw-lal') to howl with a wailing tone, to yell with a boisterous one." "And cry unto the Lord" – cry is the Hebrew word

Zaaq (zaw-ak) to shriek from anguish or danger. To most of God's children this is foreign.

As we enter in intercession, the Holy Spirit will begin to deal with us about ourselves, different areas in our lives, his holiness, purity, and sanctification. If you plan on having prayer power and authority in your life from God, you must realize that you can't live just any kind of way. God will began to touch areas in your life concerning pride, jesting, lying, compromising, speaking the truth at all times, etc. He will restrain you from doing certain things that others do. You will not be allowed. For example: Many Christians are going to the movie theater at anytime to watch anything or watch anything on television and feel free about it. But when you have totally given your whole life to Christ, you can't do that. There is a restraint from doing a lot of things. I am not saying that going to the movie theatre is wrong. I want to ask you this question. Is what you are feeding your spirit to the edification of the body? Is it bringing glory to God? Or ask yourself this question. Am I growing to become a better person? Is what I am feeding my spirit affecting anyone positively or negatively? How much affect is this having on me mentally or emotionally? I feel this warning signal go off within my spirit and a tugging that I just don't feel released to go and see a particular movie. Maybe this is a poor example, but I want to be as simple and plain as I can so that you can get the picture. Many times, God has spoken to me and said, what others do, you yourself will not be able to do because of his dealings in my life, and because of what he has called me to do.

As an intercessor, God will deal with you about telling jokes about people, mocking, or things that are not true, which are lies. For example: say someone you knew was 60 years old and you introduced them to another person. Your friend was asked how old he was, and laughingly your friend said that he was 50 years old. Shockingly, the person looked puzzled because he was seeing one thing and hearing another. So playfully, your friend finally admits that he was only kidding, and that he was 60 years old. Now in God's sight, he was standing there lying, and by you standing there laughing along with them and not speaking the truth, you have become a partaker of that lie. You see, God is a Holy God, a pure, unspotted God. He is righteous, and in him you will find nothing that defiles. He wants his bride to be the same, for his Word says to be Holy, for our temples to be Holy (I Pet. 1:15-16; 3:16-17; 2 Cor. 7:1; Ephesians 1:4). The closer you get to God's Holiness, the more purging will be done. In this you will see that you are truly not your own but you are the Lord's (I Cor. 6:19-20; Rom. 14:7-8). Then you will say as Jesus said, "not my will, but God, your will be done." There is a price to be paid. All the Lord asks is that we love him enough to say, "yes Lord, yes to your will, and to your call with a sincere heart."

D. The Importance of Intercessory Prayer

It is good to know the scriptures from Genesis to Revelation, for it is God's Word that we must live by. However, when you are interceding, the Holy Spirit must give the right scripture to pray concerning that situation. That prayer must be unctioned (guided) by the Holy Spirit in order for the Holy Spirit to be able to do its job. We must not use our intellect or just pick a scripture to pray, but allow the Holy Spirit to show us what particular scripture he wants prayed at that time (Ephesians 6:18; Rom. 2:26-27; Jude 20-21). It is not in the eloquence of words, or how long, but is through the unction and direction of the Holy Spirit which will bring forth the prayer that is needed at the time that is needed.

Jesus only prayed the prayers that were the heart of his father. We, as intercessors must pray only the prayers that are the heartbeat of the Father. When we do, God's anointing is there to break the shackles and bondages, to lose the bound, to bring forth salvation, healing, deliverance, and guidance to the people. We must learn this, for it is very vital and important for us to know. The Holy Spirit knows what we should pray and will make intercession through us. Allow the Holy Spirit to direct you. Don't just pick a scripture to pray for that person, ask the Holy Spirit to give you what to pray for that particular need so that you won't be praying amiss. The Lord wants to govern our prayer life. He wants us to yield our prayer life over to him, so that he can teach us the proper way of praying. For example, I was asked to pray, by a dear sister, that God would give her a husband. Now, I could have just started praying that God will supply this young lady with a husband, but in my spirit I sensed that the Lord wanted her to draw closer to him. He wanted her to build an intimate relationship with the Father. So I prayed according to the guidance of the Holy Spirit, that the Holy Spirit would woo her to himself so that she could grow in God and learn to know his voice. I also prayed that in his timing, he would bring her the mate that he wanted her to have. Two years later, she was married to a lovely Christian brother. She had grown in those two years to know and love the Lord in a much deeper realm before she married.

Yield yourselves to God so that the work can be accomplished. God wants to be Savior, Lord, Master, and Ruler in our lives. He is looking for obedient servants.

Before we can truly stand in the gap for anyone, we must truly love one another. We must see our brother as ourselves. We must place ourselves in his place and feel what he feels (being sensitized by the Holy Spirit to identify). The enemy of men's souls is powerless against intercessory prayer. When the Holy Spirit prays through us, we can be sure that the prayer is pure, and not tainted.

When the burden of the Lord comes upon you, it is a supernatural experience, wherein, God is allowing us to feel his grief, pain, sorrow, and love. As we stay close to God, we will know his heartbeat and our hearts will be broken with the things that breaks his heart.

In the Spirit, we will find it easy to love our enemies and only then can we pray in the spirit of love for a difficult person. But then we are not praying with our own natural understanding, or even our own feelings, but with the perfect love of God.

God is looking for someone to stand in the gap for his people, this nation, and other countries. We must be willing to lay down our lives for others; for when you are standing in the gap on another's behalf, you are literally laying your life down in order that another life may be renewed. You are taking on the pain and hurt of another, and praying them through to victory. God is looking for people who will say, "Lord, I'm willing to stand in the gap, to lay my life down at the altar for another, use me for this purpose, Lord." Will you stand in the gap? (Jer. 9:17-20; Joel 1:13-14; 2:12-17).

In these later days before the Lord's coming, God is going to move by his Spirit in realms that we have not seen. The greater works shall be seen (John 14:12).

Chapter IV

GOD'S LABORERS OF LOVE

I John 3:16 – Hereby perceive we the love of God, because he laid down his life for us: and we ought to lay down our lives for the brethren.

The greatest and highest expression of Love is self-sacrifice. Let's look at the meaning of self-sacrifice. It is sacrifice of oneself or one's interest for others or for a cause or idea. This is what Jesus did for us. He was our sacrifice. In I John 3:17-18, it states – "But whoso hath this world's good, and seeth his brother have need, and shutteth up his bowels of compassion from him, how dwelleth the love of God in him? My little children, let us not love in word, neither in tongue; but in deed and in truth." Jesus saw our need in every area of our lives, and he has whole heartedly, without any reservation, met our every need. In St. John 17:3, Jesus made intercession for us. Jesus was concerned about us knowing the Father. I believe that in the 17th chapter of John, there is the most enlighten prayer that I have ever read. He loved us so much that he poured out his bowels of love for us in prayer to the

Father. We are his friends because he laid down his life for us (John 15:13; 3:16). In that chapter, Jesus had a "love feast" with the Father. The love and intimacy Jesus has with the Father is like no other love we know. What a bond and respect they have with each other.

When he was at the garden of Gethsemane, he poured out his soul unto the Father. He loved the Father so much that, he wanted the will of his Father to be done in his life. He loved us so much that, he yielded to the Father's will, to die so that all mankind could have life. Oh, what a labor of love he showed toward us (Matt. 26:36-44). We must "will" to love each other as Christ loves us. We must be willing to be laborers of love so that the world around us will see and know that we are of God. Love heals, comforts, breaks shackles in people's lives, and will cause the weeds in our lives to disappear. Just think what the world would be like if we all became laborers of love. The Song of Solomon says that, "love is as strong as death. Many waters cannot quench love, neither can the floods drown it" (Sol. 8:6-7). In I John 4:7-8 it tells us "to love one another, for love is of God; and everyone that loveth is born of God, and knoweth God. He that loveth not knoweth not God; for God is love." Love is an action. The scripture tells us not to love in words, neither in tongue; but in deed and in truth (I John 3:18). And hereby we know that we are of the truth, and shall assure our hearts before him. For if our heart condemn us, God is greater than our heart, and knoweth all things. Beloved, if our heart condemn us not, then have we confidence toward God. And whatsoever we ask, we receive of him, because we keep his commandments, and do those things that are pleasing in his sight (I John 3:19-22).

God's love never dies, it increases. You can't buy it at any price because it is priceless. Jesus's love for us is priceless. No matter how much the devil tried, Jesus would not sell out because he loved us.

As I stated before, every blow that he took was because he loved us. Every stripe that he bore was because of love. Every unkind word and every tear that he shed was because of love. Every day that he fasted and prayed was because of love. Everything that he went through was because he loved us. His love was unconditional and everlasting.

I see a mother holding her child in her arms, cuddling the child, and expressing to that little one how much she loves him. In this same way I can see the Father, "Abba Father," looking at us. Lovingly, He takes us in his arms and wraps his arms around us saying, "my little child, oh how I love you. I will love you and protect you always." Oh, praise the Lord. Thank you Father for your unconditional love.

We, as intercessors, must love as He loves. We have the lover living inside of us, for He is love. We have the giver living inside of us because he gave. We have the originator living inside of us; for he created all things and spoke them into existence. Jesus gave himself to his father and loved unconditionally. How much more should we exemplify his love. We must be God's laborers of love. We must be expressions of that love here on earth. Say yes to his will. Be used as a laborer of love. Be a representative of His healing power.

Chapter V

IDENTIFICATION AND AGONY

Romans 15:1 – "We then that are strong ought to bear the infirmities of the weak, and not to please ourselves."

One book that I would recommend to you to read is Rees Howells Intercessor by Norman Grubb. When I was recommended to read the book, I couldn't understand why. As I read the book, it identified so much with what the Lord had told me to do, and what the Holy Spirit was teaching me. I thought that I was strange because I knew no one else that was going through what I was or being used the same way in prayer, not until I read Norman Grubb's book. I was a minister of the gospel as well as a worship leader in the church that I grew up in as a Christian. I had ministered for about two and a half to three years and lead worship for five years. One day in prayer at our church, the Holy Spirit said to me, "Carolyn, I do not want you to preach or lead worship right now. I want you to stick to intercessory prayer because there are a lot of things that I want to show you and teach you in the realm of the Spirit that you would not learn standing behind a pulpit or leading worship. I had to step down. When I told my pastor what the Lord had said, he could not understand, because he had never heard of it before. Neither had I until a deacon at Halpine Baptist Church recommended that I buy Norman Grubb's book on intercession. I thank God for that deacon because he was used of God to help guide me into what the Holy Spirit wanted me to do and to bring me to an understanding of why He had me doing certain things concerning identification. A lot of times the Lord would have me eating a certain type of food for a while so that I could identify with the people of a certain country for whom I would be praying. Many times I would experience things because of whom I would be praying for who was experiencing the same thing. I would be interceding for that person until that person was released from that situation. I had to intercede and do warfare on that person's behalf. Once I was released, I knew that the person that I was interceding and doing warfare for was released. I know this might sound strange to some of you, but this is exactly what happened. It is called identification. I had to know exactly what that person was going through by experiencing it myself. Let us look at the meaning of identification. It is to identify with the ones you are praying for, the act of identity. You submerge your interest in their needs and sufferings, as far as the Holy Spirit allows you to take their place in prayer. Jesus identified with Mary and Martha in the death of Lazarus. Jesus identified with us (Phil. 2:7-8). Before Jesus could give his life up, He had to identify with us in order to see the complete reason for redemption.

In order for them to be released out of that situation, I had to be willing to stand in the gap in order for complete healing and deliverance to be released.

I had to feel the pain and suffering in order for me to pray through for their deliverance. This is called agony. For example: My niece had to have open heart surgery. We did not know that her heart had a large hole in it. I noticed that I began to feel week, and I begin to feel her chest pains even before we knew she had the problem. I felt as though I was going to have a heart attack. I went to a heart specialist for him to check my heart out. He did all sorts of tests but found no reason for the pain. No, it wasn't indigestion. I knew then that I was carrying her pains. After she was admitted into the hospital, I asked the Lord to allow me to take her pain for her. This is the extensiveness of standing in the gap for someone. It goes further than we really understand. It is more than standing in a prayer line, on behalf of another for prayer. I went through that time as if I was having problems. I felt the pain for my niece and she went through the heart surgery with not as much suffering and pain as she would have had I not offered myself to stand in the gap for her. The doctors had stated that it was a miracle that she was alive because of the size of the hole that was in her heart and the loss of blood. The blood was just going through the hole and flowing out from the hole. God knew what was going on and He knew that had I not been obedient to turn down my plate and stand in the gap for my niece, she would not be alive today. The surgeons could not believe that she was alive with the extensiveness of her conditions. She was born with the hole in her heart and it was not detected until she was 12 years old. What was supposed to be a four hour surgery turned out to be a six hours. She had lost so much blood before she was diagnosed that the doctors couldn't believe that she was alive. All that the Lord needed was a willing vessel to stand in the gap for someone in serious need.

Moses identified with the people of Israel. He interceded on the people's behalf and asked the Lord to forgive them for the sin that they had committed. Moses had no part in the sin of idolatry but he identified with the people. He loved the people so much that he laid down his life before the Lord and stated, "Yet now, if thou wilt forgive their sin, and if not, blot me, I pray thee, out of thy book which thou hast written (Ex. 32:31-33). We see how that Aaron wore the ephod, and on the ephod laid a breastplate with the 12 tribes of Israel written on it. Aaron presented the children of Israel before the Lord in the Holy Place of the tabernacle and presented each tribe on the ephod up to the Lord for the forgiveness of their sins (Ex. 39:1-43). Esther and her handmaidens interceded and fasted before the Lord and all the Jews of Shusan for three days and nights that the Lord would spare her people from destruction. She identified with her people. She not only identified with them but loved them as well, to the point of dying if necessary (Esther 4:16). Jeremiah was grieved in his spirit because of the idolatry of Israel and made intercession for Israel. He asked that the Lord would only pour out His anger on the heathen that knew not God, and the families that called not on the name of the Lord (Jer. 10:19-25). There are many more who interceded on their people's behalf, Ezekiel, Solomon, Daniel, and so on.

In Isaiah 53:12, it states that Jesus "poured out his soul until death, and He was numbered with the transgressors, and He bore the sins of many, and made intercession" for the transgressors. What greater person to show us identification with the ones he interceded for. What greater love can be shown?

My mother had a number of strokes at various times, but on this particular day of July 1990, two weeks before I was to leave for Nairobi, Kenya, in East Africa, she had another stroke and it was worse. She had lost her memory, her left hand was paralyzed, her mouth twisted and she was in a coma. The doctors stated that she would be in the hospital for a while and then even if she improved a little, she would be in a vegetable state and would not improve. I was told before I arrived home to see my mother, that she had a couple of small strokes while she was in the hospital. I went home to see my mother, and the Holy Spirit told me to anoint her head with oil and to just pray in the spirit. The Holy Spirit said to me that I was not to speak a word of English until he instructed me to. I did as I was instructed, and when I poured the anointing oil (oil that I had prayed over in prayer) upon her head and touch her forehead to pray, I began to see in the spirit what demons had a hold of her. I prayed in the spirit, and took authority over those demons and began to curse them to the root, and commanded them to loose my mother's brain cells and her body and to go to a dry place and stay there. As I prayed, my mother screamed as though someone was literally pulling her hair out from the roots. Now remember, I had my hand on her forehead lightly. All of a sudden she could speak some. She told my sister that I was pulling her hair out from the roots. You see, as I began to curse those evil spirits that had a hold of my mother, they were coming out from her head and it felt as though someone was literally pulling her hair out. I left that Monday to come back to Maryland, only to hear more disturbing news. I had only a few more days before I was to leave America to go to Nairobi. It was on Thursday morning of that last week of July 1990, that the Holy Spirit spoke to me and told me to stay home and intercede for my mom and do warfare on her behalf. People of God, let me tell you what our God did for my mom. I called to my office and told them I would not be in that day because I had some very important business to take care of. It was true. I had important business with the Holy Spirit in prayer. I lay prostrate on the floor beside my bed and began to pray as never before for my mom. I am telling you the truth that as I was praying in the spirit, my language changed. I was taken in the spirit by the Holy Spirit to Benin City, Nigeria. I saw Bishop Benson Idahosa praying for my mom and calling her by her name (Mary). I heard him as clear as I would hear someone standing in front of me speaking. He took authority over the enemy and cursed them. As he was speaking in English, I was praying with the same power and authority. As he finished praying for my mom, I started praying for him in English. People of God, this really happened. We cannot say what the Holy Spirit will and will not do because we do not comprehend, nor understand the depth of God's love for his people. We do not understand what depth the Holy Spirit will go to see one of his own set free. I have learned this through prayer. It is not based on what we have been taught about prayer because most of the time the one that is doing the teaching has not allowed the Holy Spirit to take them into the deeper depths in the Spirit. It must be an unselfish love for souls before the Holy Spirit will allow you to be used this way. You must be willing to lay your life down if necessary, so that the person will be set free. I know that this sounds to the extreme, but listen to me. The Holy Spirit will lead you and guide you in all truth. We must have confidence in the Holy Spirit and the Lord that the Lord will not allow anything to happen to us while we are taking care of what he want us to do in prayer. The next day, early in the morning, I received a phone call from my mom. I was in awe of what the Lord and the Holy Spirit did for my mom. While the Holy Spirit was praying through Bishop Benson Idahosa and me, the Holy Spirit visited my mother's hospital room, touched her limbs, her brain, her heart, and her mouth and totally brought her back from the dead. My mother said that all of sudden she could talk and with the aid of a walker she could walk. She said that there was no paralysis, and that her speech and mind was clear. Praise the Lord. God gave my mother a miracle. My mother said that very instantly she felt fine. She was walking down the hall on her floor in the hospital. She was a walking miracle. My God can deliver if we are willing to pay the price in prayer. I know that there may be some critics out there that may speak against what I am saying, but God did it, and the proof was my mom. She was to be in the hospital for two months, and then would have to be sent to a nursing home. I told the Lord that I couldn't go to Africa and preach about his delivering power, when my mother needed his delivering touch. My Father showed his love and his concern for my mother and he also knew that I needed to be free to minister without any hindrances. Let us take the limits off of God. Our theology, and the doctrine of men, will hinder the move of God. God honors his Word, not our theology or our doctrine. We say that he can heal, deliver and set free, but do we really believe it. Put aside our theology, which is tainted with human opinions and ideas, and let us begin to believe God with childlike faith that he is more than able to deliver, more than able to heal, more than able to save, and more than able to touch with his finger and restore. I have seen the mighty hand of God move in people's lives just because of unselfish love to lay oneself down in prayer and stand in the gap for that soul. God will move, he will heal, and he will answer if we just only believe, for without faith, it is impossible to please the Lord.

We must identify with that person's need, ache and pain, and in order to do that, we must love enough to lay down our life if need be. We must have an ear to hear what the Spirit of the Lord is saying about that person. We must be willing to lay down our lives for the brethren. Are you willing?

Chapter VI

THE POWER OF THE TONGUE

As I have walked with the Lord in intercession, he has shown me that he must have the control of my tongue. James, chapter 3 states that the tongue is a little member, and boasteth great things. Behold, how great a matter a little fire kindleth. And the tongue is a fire, a world of iniquity: so is the tongue among our members, that it defileth the whole body, and setteth on fire the course of nature, and it is set on fire of hell. But the tongue can no man tame, it is an unruly evil, full of deadly poison (James 3:5-6, 8). As Christians, we must yield that member of our body to the Lord. We must be very careful that we do not offend, curse or cause one of our brethren to stumble or backslide. "But whosoever shall offend one of these little ones which believe in me, it were better for him that a millstone were hanged about his neck, and that he were drowned in the depth of the sea" (Matt. 18:6). All of us are on different levels in the Lord and should walk circumspectly. We are so quick to judge our sister or brother just because they are different. We all have different personalities and we all have different ways of doing things. If a person is different, inquire of the Father, and I guarantee you that he will tell you. Be very careful of the words that come out of your mouth. What you say could cause a brother or sister to give up on the Lord altogether. In all of our lives there are areas that we have not yielded to the Lord, and it will take the Holy Spirit to show them that area. We should pray for that brother and sister that they may be strengthened and made whole and complete in that area of his or her life.

God gives you discernment to see an area in which a person is weak, and God actually speaks to you to speak to that person God will show you at that moment exactly what to say that will bring about Godly results. I have seen so much damage done to the body of Christ in this area. I have heard slurs and seen stones thrown, even across the pulpit from leaders, to the people of God and this should not be. This grieves God and the Holy Spirit. We must confess our faults ("our own") to each other, and pray one for another, that we may be healed. "The effectual fervent prayer of a righteous man availeth much" (James 5:16).

The body of Christ is a wounded body. How? When we bite and devour one another with our tongue. As intercessors, we have so much for which to intercede. Let us not give up now. Pray without ceasing for the wounded body of Christ; pray in the Holy Ghost. We need to turn down our plates and begin to fast and pray for each other. We need each other. We must see that we, as the body of Christ, must stand together and fight a good fight in the Spirit. Let us stop yielding ourselves to the enemy to be used of him to tear one another down. We must stop yielding our tongue to the devil to cut and destroy one another, but yield our tongue over to the Holy Spirit to be a blessing and not a cursing.

Let us see what Proverbs says about the tongue. Proverbs 10:19 states, "In the multitude of words there wanteth not sin: but he that refraineth his lips is wise." Proverbs 15:4 states that, "a wholesome tongue is a tree of life: but perverseness therein is a breach in the spirit." A wholesome tongue literally means a tongue that speaks life and healing. A breach in the spirit is a crushing of the spirit. Don't speak rashly. Don't thrust out damaging words, but speak life, speak healing to each other. Oh, how devastating to crush the spirit of a person. Oh Lord, forgive all of us, including myself, for speaking out of anger back at someone that has been crushed by what we have said. Think how you have felt when this happened to you. A crushed spirit is a wound that takes time to heal. Some have turned away from the faith, or have stopped attending church altogether. They have become withdrawn from Christians and they cannot trust another pastor or minister of the gospel. Do you see how serious this is? Proverbs 18:21 states that, "Death and life are in the power of the tongue: and they that love it shall eat the fruit thereof." Proverbs 13:3 – "He that keepeth his mouth keepeth his life; but he that openeth wide his lips shall have destruction." Proverbs 21:23 states that, "whosoever keepeth his mouth and his tongue keepeth his soul from troubles." You may ask, how can we keep our soul from troubles? By keeping our mouth shut.

Let's look at Matthew 12:36-37. Matthew states that we will be held accountable for every idle word that comes from our lips in the day of judgment. The words that we speak, that are not pure, places us in trouble with our Father and by those same words bringeth forth trouble with each other. Let every man be swift to hear, slow to speak, slow to wrath: for the wrath of man worketh not the righteousness of God (James 1:19-20). If we want to see good days in our lives, then let us refrain our tongues from evil, and let no guile come forth through our lips (I Peter 3:10). Instead let us turn aside from evil, and do good; let us seek peace, and pursue it. For the eyes of the Lord are over the righteous, and his ears are open unto their prayers: but the face of the Lord is against them that do evil (I Peter 3:11-12).

Intercessors, let us not yield our tongues to do evil, but to do good, so that the Lord will hear our prayers. Let us not grieve the Holy Spirit and break our Father's heart. From this day forward, let us give our tongue to the Lord, and glorify God.

"Father, I pray that as intercessors, we learn the danger of the misuse of our tongue. Help us to overcome evil with good. Teach us, so that we will be able to teach others. Purge us from all that is not pure, and wash us, and we shall be whiter than snow. Please forgive us for using our tongue as a weapon to hurt others in anger. Forgive us for not recognizing that this is not pleasing to you. We give you our tongue that you will help us to use this little member of our body to glorify you. You said in your word that that the tongue no man can tame. Forgive us for ignoring the Holy Spirit when he was trying to get our attention. We want to walk in humility and integrity. Bring total deliverance to us so that we will not hurt others with our words that comes out of our mouths. Lord we thank you for your love, grace and mercy, that you have given to us. For if you did not love us, we would have never known the sin that we had committed. We thank you for showing us our shortcomings and for forgiving us. We love you with a steadfast love, always." Amen.

Chapter VII

THE CALL

Come up higher, higher and higher,
Come up higher, higher in me;
Come sup at my table that I have prepared for thee;
Just yield to me, yield to me,
That I may impart my grace unto thee;
Look and see, look and see,
Look and see what I have done for thee;
Walk in my power, my Holy power;
Look and see, look what I have done for thee;
That you may know that I am with thee,
Come up higher, higher and higher
Come up higher, higher in me;
Draw closer to me, closer to me,
That you may know me in my Holiness;
That you may know my will for your life today;
Come sup with me in your prayer closets,
That you may find strength in the time of need;

Strength to do battle, battle indeed,
Battle in the spirit, as the whole world will see,
They will see my glory in thee.

At the end of the day, after finishing chapter 6, I asked the lord to show me how I could end the book. As I was standing at the Silver Spring Metro Bus Stop, the Lord began to birth a new song into my spirit, a prophetic song. As I sang the song, I realized that this was not just an ordinary song. The Holy Spirit directed me to write the words down as I sang the song. I was amazed that the Holy Spirit would give me the ending for the book in this fashion. How marvelous and wonderful the Lord has shown his infinite wisdom and glory. The Holy Spirit said, "this is for the last chapter of the book, write it down. I pray that the Lord will meet you, wherever you are in him, in intercessory prayer. May God be glorified through this book, and may souls draw closer to his bosom, as they enter into their secret closets to dine at the Master's table.

THE END

"Jesus counted not his own life dear to him, for he laid down his life for the sheep" (John 10:15-18).

CPSIA information can be obtained
at www.ICGtesting.com
Printed in the USA
LVHW071527090623
749237LV00003B/34